JUDY YOUNG OCKO / M. L. ROSENBLUM

*YOU'RE
THE
SECRET
INGREDIENT
IN
GOOD ADS*

ADVERTISING

HANDBOOK

FOR RETAIL

MERCHANTS

FOREWORD

It's crucial that buyers, merchants and advertising personnel maintain a good working relationship. Yet, all too often, each attempts to achieve similar goals by pulling in different directions. This is costly.

The purpose of this book is to give the merchandising side a better understanding of the advertising side. Hopefully, this renewed understanding will enable each to merchandise better and promote better.

Our authors open Chapter 1 with a very true thought: "Advertising does not start in the Advertising Department. It starts when you're in the market . . . buying."

Since a great deal of money is spent in the promotion of your store, it is hoped that this book will be read, re-read and passed along from department to department. It's through better departmental understanding and early planning that sales goals are achieved.

John A. Murphy, Vice President
Sales Promotion Division
National Retail Merchants Association

"The National Retail Merchants Association which represents the world's leading department and specialty stores, is devoted to research and education in general merchandise retailing"

Published by Sales Promotion Division
National Retail Merchants Association
100 West 31st Street   New York, N.Y. 10001

TABLE OF CONTENTS

INTRODUCTION

INTRODUCTION

This book grew out of a talk to a merchandise clinic. The response was so tremendous we decided there was a void that needed filling.

When we started to think about it, we realized why. Both of us do a lot of lectures and clinics and consultations for advertising groups . . . and often go home feeling that we've been talking to the wrong people. Sure, we can give them a little insight, a little inspiration, share our ideas and our skills. But it's like talking to ourselves. The ad people are not really the ones who need the message. They have it. You are, because you . . . the merchants . . . are the secret ingredient of good advertising. Unfortunately, it's a rarely used ingredient.

It's not all your fault. We, who are in the business of communication, have somehow failed to communicate to you exactly what your role is in the creation of advertising; what you should be involved in, what you should leave to us. It's a subject that's rarely discussed and, as far as we know, has never been the subject of a book. Which is where we come in. We think our book will surprise you. It may even shake you up. But we're sure it will help you get better advertising.

Judy Young Ocko
Morris L. Rosenblum

POSTSCRIPT

January, 1981

A book is never finished. As it goes into the marketplace, you discover that some subjects have been treated too briefly. Or new areas of interest, like marketing, have suddenly become important. Which is why this book has just been revised and expanded. With the basic knowledge intact, but updated. And with the basic purpose still intact: to help the merchant understand advertising and his role in it.

CHAPTER 1

THE MERCHANT AND HIS ADS: RESPONSIBILITIES

Advertising does not start in the advertising department.

It starts when you're in the market . . . buying.

You do your job as well as you know how. You get merchandising advice from every source you can. You get marketing advice, media advice. Then you schedule an ad.

You open your newspaper . . . and there it is. Your dumb, dull ad, with maybe one-tenth the pulling power it should have had.

Why?

What good does all the advice do you if you don't communicate to the customers? If you don't stop them, sell them, and bring them into your store?

Why are so many retail ads faceless? With no personality of their own.

Why are so many ads a waste of expensive real estate . . . and the way newspaper rates are these days, space is very expensive real estate, indeed.

Why do so many ads not only fail to convince customers, but even make it harder for them to shop?

Because most merchants don't know how to use the advertising department, that's why.

In the usual table of organization of a store, the ad department is a service department, but there's a unique mutual interdependence between merchants and advertising that's rarely appreciated.

Merchants don't seem to realize how vital they are to the creation of good advertising. They often seem to think ads just happen.

1

This is typical of what merchants all too often do. A buyer gets a call to provide information for an ad or to OK an ad. The buyer is busy, very busy. So he dispatches his new assistant assistant. Eager, of course, but ignorant of what makes a good ad. And there he is . . . coming through the door of the advertising department: the instant advertising expert.

It's like asking the sugeon's receptionist to do an appendectomy.

You, as a merchant, have certain responsibilities in the creation of advertising. Your job is not finished when you select the merchandise and schedule an ad. It's not finished when you write your information sheet. It's only finished when you have finally signed off a proof and the ad is ready for insertion.

It's a responsibility too big to trust to anyone else.

This may sound like strong language, but it's a sure way of getting better advertising.

Of course, the advertising department has its responsibilities, too. What are the responsibilities of the merchant and the advertising department? Unfortunately, they're not something that can be put into a simple list . . . you do this and I'll do that . . . which will be valid for all stores at all times.

There are stores where the advertising department selects the merchandise. There are stores where the buyer information sheets literally become the copy for the ad. There are stores where, instead of working together as a team, the advertising department and the merchants have a constant tug of war, each trying to get as much power as possible. Which is not the way good advertising is created.

Most stores, however, would agree that the following division of labor is fair, equitable, and workable.

The merchant

Selects the merchandise for the ad.
Schedules the ad.
Provides the facts.
Provides merchandise for layout and art.
Explains where merchandise emphasis should be.
Does the basic arithmetic (percentages off, etc.).

Gives the customer benefits.
Points out any legal problems (trade-marks and such).
Reads proofs carefully.
Checks art, copy, prices to make sure facts are correct.

Advertising department

Translates facts into customer language, from customer point of view.
Dramatizes (not exaggerates) the merchandise.
Gives the reasons for buying . . . at your store.
Adds urge to action.
Does copy, layout, art . . . in store style.
Designates type.
Marks up ad and sends to newspaper.
Corrects proofs.
Releases ad to newspaper.

Most merchandise and advertising people would agree on this list. But it's only the beginning, the black and white. There are many gray areas where decisions should be made jointly. How much merchandise in the ad? Art or no art? If the featured item is not graphic, would the ad be more successful with a more dramatic item substituted? Could the ad be smaller? Should it be bigger? Would it be better if related merchandise strewn through the newspaper were put into a single, bigger ad? Would a lot of unrelated merchandise be better broken into individual ads?

Maybe you always thought these were the buyer's decisions. Maybe you thought it was the advertising department's. It's neither. You'll get a sounder decision if you and the advertising department work it out together.

3

CHAPTER 2
WHAT IS A GOOD AD?

The answer is very simple.

A good ad is one that sells. That sells merchandise, sells an idea, sells your store. This is true whether you're screaming one-day sale or saluting the Community Chest.

A good ad persuades, convinces, and urges people into action. It answers all the reader's unspoken questions, from what will it do for me to can I afford it to can I charge it.

A good ad must catch the reader's eye . . . and keep it on the page until your message is absorbed. According to research on the subject, you have precisely 3 seconds to stop the reader. If you don't do it then, the page is turned and you might as well not be in the newspaper.

A good ad must be attractive, it must be easy to read, it must tell customers that what you're selling will do something for them. In advertising circles, this is known as "the customer benefit". It will make them look more fashionable, make them look better, make life pleasanter or easier, their homes nicer, their kids happier, save them money, or even make the neighbors envious. It can be as elementary as a sofa that won't stain or as complex as a mink coat for a young woman that says . . . see, I've made it!

Above all, a good ad must be news. It must present timely merchandise. The language should be today's. Not way out (you'll turn off more customers than you turn on) but it shouldn't be old-fashioned either. Who goes around "garbed in fashion" in the 20th century? In some ads, they do!

The graphics must also be of today: clean, simple, yet dramatic.

A good ad must be honest. It should dramatize, not exaggerate. It should contain no false claims, no hyperbole, no superlatives you

4

can't justify. This is even more important now when the BBB, the FTC, and assorted consumer groups are ready to pounce on you.

A good ad should not only be honest with the customer, but you must be honest with yourself as well.

If you're looking for young customers, kicky advertising won't help you, unless you have the merchandise the youngsters want . . . in depth.

If you're a promotional store, don't try to make your advertising look like that of an exclusive salon. You're only kidding yourself . . . and bewildering your customers. The woman who never spends more than ten bucks for a handbag will be afraid to come in. The woman who can afford to pay three figures for a handbag might come through your door . . . once.

A good ad not only reflects your store, but it should reflect your customers, their point of view, their way of life.

Just as your merchandise does.

Most of all, a good ad must be your store's ad, immediately identified as your ad . . . even if you didn't have a logotype.

This is a lot to ask of an ad. No wonder we need your help!

Naturally, a good sale ad, a good non-sale ad, and a good institutional ad are not the same because their objectives are different.

A good sale ad must sell the savings *and* the goods. Remember, you're not selling price alone. You're selling something *at* a price. Who wants celluloid collars . . . even at a penny each?

A good sale ad must be convincing. The trick of sale advertising is to make customers feel they're getting more than they paid for. Give them a reason for a sale . . . your anniversary or a special purchase because a manufacturer was loaded or whatever . . . and you'll sell them.

A good sale ad should have customers with their cash and/or credit cards in their hands lining up at your door. If the merchandise is right. If the price is right. If the ad is convincing.

Indirect, non-sale advertising can't be measured quite that easily. It depends on your objectives.

If you're trying to attract a new customer (young people, working women, etc.), the first few ads may produce very little. Then, gradually, as you have sold your audience, they'll produce more. If you're trying to establish yourself as a fashion store (ready-to-wear or home furnishings), an idea store, a service store, the going will probably be equally slow. But this kind of advertising is often essential, a good investment in the future of your store.

You shouldn't try to measure the result of an individual ad, but look at the bottom line at the end of the year.

A good institutional should remind people of what you stand for, or make them proud to be your customers . . . or both.

It should not be overtly boastful. Instead, like any good ad, it should tell me what you're doing for me. For my shopping convenience, my shopping pleasure. For my community. For my favorite charity.

Here results aren't even measurable in years, but in decades.

You may not think that, as a merchant, you're directly involved in institutionals. You may shrug them off as that Merry Christmas ad or those salutes to the garden club ladies. Yet some of the best ways to institutionalize a store come out of merchandise.

When you run an assortment ad, you're running a baby institutional: telling people what a wide choice they have at your store. When you open a new department. When you bring them real fashion news. When you bring them fashion news at a price. Everything a store stands for is institutional . . . whether it's in a merchandise ad or an institutional ad.

What most people don't realize, and this often includes advertising creators, is that every ad is an institutional in its way. Every ad. Because every ad tells your audience so much about the kind of store you are. From price points to taste level.

How can you make sure your ads are good ads?

Read on.

CHAPTER 3
COPY: WHAT THE ADVERTISING DEPARTMENT
NEEDS FROM YOU

Let's talk about the words. Where do they come from? They come out of the facts. *Your* facts.

The better the input, the better the ad. And when we say better, we mean more effective.

We don't create ads out of air. Copywriters don't sit at their electric typewriters or video terminals waiting for inspiration.

A writer takes your facts and translates them into consumer language, from the consumer point of view, giving all the consumer benefits.

That's our job.

But only the merchant knows why the merchandise was bought. Surely not to fill empty racks. There's a reason, a story, behind every purchase. Why don't you tell us?

Let us give you an example.

We were once involved in creating a special group of floor covering sale ads for Macy's.

One of them was a Rya rug sale. The information sheet came up with "Special Purchase. Our Lowest Price ever for a wool pile Rya rug." True, the price was good. The merchandise was good. But in our marketing area, as fast as one store dropped its price on Ryas, other stores dropped theirs even lower.

Instead of building our ad on the lowest price story, we sat down with the merchants and started firing questions at them. Only to discover this was, indeed, a very special purchase. A manufacturer was switching from wool to synthetics because wool was getting too expensive and we'd bought up all his wool rugs.

7

Our headline: *"With wool going up the way it is, how can Macy's put such extraordinary prices on these all-wool pile Ryas? Simple . . . for Macy's. Denmark's top Rya maker switched to synthetics. He offered us every wool pile rug he had. We took them. And put mad, marvelous prices on every one!"*

The result: a near sell-out.

The question remains. Why weren't we told these facts? Why did we have to dig them out? A less experienced writer with less time would not have learned the story behind the special purchase. And the same merchandise at the same price might have bombed.

Only the merchant can give us these stories. Why don't you?

Only the merchant can tell us the precise market for the merchandise. Why don't you?

Only the merchant can tell us which points to emphasize. Why don't you? If you say "drip-dry flowered shirts with long sleeves", you're not telling us where to put the emphasis in our ad. Easy care? Flowers? Long sleeves? The shirt? Which is the important fashion point? Only you know. We don't ask you to write the ad (more about that later, a lot more) but to provide the facts on which a good ad can be built.

You see, a writer writes many departments and can't be an expert in all of them. We're not merchants. (Although good copywriters often become good merchants, too.) And the smaller your advertising department, the more kinds of merchandise we have to write. So make sure the writer has every fact, in the order of their importance.

The writer won't use all of them, of course. But they start the creative juices working.

We need all the facts

In today's climate of consumerism, the more facts you give, the more convincing your ad sounds. And it's a better ad. We take too much for granted on the part of the customer.

You know exactly how big a queen size mattress is, but the customer, who hasn't bought a mattress in 10 years . . . and is switching from a double bed . . . doesn't.

You know that u-neck or v-neck or some-sort-of-neck is big in men's sweaters. But do men? Only some. Your ads must tell them.

Many years ago, when women still wore housedresses, instead of pants, to mop the kitchen floor, a writer was doing a small ad on percale housedresses. The information sheet provided colors and sizes and styles and prices. After all, a housedress was a housedress was a housedress. But the writer asked the buyer for more facts. And got them. Including the fact that there were 180 threads to every square inch of the percale. That's a lot of little threads to an inch . . . and sounds like fine quality. The writer was impressed and built the ad around that fact. The store had to re-order three times . . . just for that ad.

But it's a sad story anyway. Because every housedress maker, every buyer knew about the percale. Yet nobody had bothered to tell the customer.

So don't take obvious facts for granted. Give them to your writer.

The facts you provide must be specific

Good advertising copy is always specific.

What, for example, does "all spring colors" mean? Pastels? Earth brown? It's pretty hot some springs.

Who buys "assorted styles of handbags"? Nobody. If you do have assorted styles, name at least some of them, so we can say "pouches, envelopes, over-the-shoulder-bags, zipped bags, and many other styles". Then the customer knows what she'll find.

If you tell me, the customer, that a chair will go in any style of room, what are you telling me? Nothing! I don't have "any style" of room. I have Provincial or Colonial or even eclectic . . . but not "any style". Spell out the styles of rooms and I identify.

Generalities are a waste of space. They don't communicate. They don't make the merchandise vivid . . . and desirable . . . to your customer.

If you have an ad full of generalities that doesn't pull well, don't blame the ad. Blame yourself for not giving the advertising department the ammunition to attract customers.

The facts should be correct, not a guess

It costs money and time to make changes and reset type. Don't invent some facts because your information sheet is due and you want to hold the space. (Sorry, we know all the tricks.) If you say blue, green, and wine . . . and they turn out to be aquamarine, avocado, and grapeberry, a whole paragraph of type will have to be reset.

If you say sale and it isn't, a whole ad must be rewritten.

You may think it's a simple matter of a few minor changes on proof . . . but there are *no* minor changes. It takes somebody's time even to change a 12.99 to 12.98 . . . and check to make sure the change has been made.

Guessing, instead of checking to make sure, can only irritate your advertising department and is hardly conducive to a good working relationship.

There's an additional hazard. If you receive only one proof from your newspaper, you never get a chance to make sure your corrections have been made properly.

You make the change on the proof. Your writer transcribes the change. The production department sends out the change. However, there's many a slip between the proof and the newspaper which the advertising department can't control. So if your TV set appears at $20 instead of $200 because you made a little last minute change, you have only yourself to fault.

The facts should be honest, not exaggerated

This has always been true. Honest facts are more convincing than unsupported (and usually unsupportable) claims.

Today, it's not just true, it's imperative. Not only are all the alphabetical agencies watching over you, but customers have become consumers.

Say that your pillows are big, fat and puffy. Mrs. Zilch orders them by mail, only to find that they're small, skinny, and deflated. You'll not only get a return, but probably a loud complaint, and maybe even a lawsuit, too.

10

Ditto if you say "Coats, up to 50% off" and Mrs. Zilch pays a baby sitter, drives 10 miles, then finds 200 coats at 15% off and exactly 3 at 50% off. This is hardly the way to make good loyal customers.

Comparative prices and percentages off have become particularly suspect. So much so that there are stores, good stores, where the buyer must sign a legal document swearing that his comparative price is correct. If it isn't, he goes job-hunting.

If you have good wanted merchandise at a good competitive price, do you really need phony comparatives?

Do you really need "our lowest price ever"? What does it mean? As far back as you can remember? Moreover, what do you do . . . next week, or next month . . . for an encore? Our lowest price ever . . . since the last time? Overkill.

Another thing customers are getting pretty sophisticated about is the dangling comparative. 25% less. Less than what? Tell them, and you'll be more convincing

Superlatives are also dangerous. If you say that this is our best mattress, what are you saying about the 10 other mattress styles you carry?

It's always better to sell the merchandise . . . and the value . . . than to try to sell big numbers and big claims. Don't underestimate your customers.

The facts should be in plain English, not technical jargon

You may know what AFC is, and if you sell radios, you'd better. But does your customer? Of course not. You'll sell more goods if you say something like "Automatic Frequency Control, so when you tune a station in, it won't drift off". If you give your writer a manufacturer's specification sheet, translate it. If you're not sure yourself, ask the manufacturer.

This is not just a hard goods problem. Ready-to-wear buyers strew their information sheets with little goodies they've picked up from "Women's Wear" and other trade sources. They need translating to the customer, too.

11

Include every customer benefit

This is your best selling tool today. What's a customer benefit? Simple. As we have explained, it's the answer to "What will this do for me?" Will it make my life easier, lovelier, will it make me more attractive . . . and so on. (See page 4.)

Here again there's a need to understand emphasis.

If you have a right-now evening fashion made of non-crush, no-iron fabric, what's the customer benefit? The big one?

If you're promoting it for wear here-and-now, the benefit is the fashion news. She'll be the most dazzling kid at the party.

If you're promoting it for travel, the benefit is the fashion news plus the non-crush.

No-iron certainly belongs in the copy, in either case, but it's not the major benefit, not headline material. Do you know any woman who ever bought an evening dress because it drip-dried?

You see, fashion itself is a consumer benefit. A fact that's often forgotten. In both wearables and durables. It says to the reader: wear me and you'll look right. Or live with me and your home will look right.

However, with something like curtains, the no-iron is as important as style. Nobody wants to iron curtains, and between the most elegant organdy that has to be ironed and the not-so-elegant that will drip-dry, today's woman will choose the no-iron.

These are obvious and simple examples.

But unless you want a headline that's merely a label, an ad that just sits there and does nothing for you, you must dig the customer benefits out of the facts and tell them to your writer. We don't know them as well as you do.

Facts: specific, correct, honest, ungarbled, with emphasis and customer benefits spelled out . . . that's what we ask of you. Why is it so hard to get? And why is it so hard to get on time?

Get your information sheets in on time

Late information is a chronic complaint of retail advertising departments. Yet, if you get your information to the ad department on time, you're more likely to end up with a good ad.

How come? We work on a tight schedule. Upset it and you'll get a routine ad because we've had no time to consider and try alternative ways of doing it. Plus, incidentally, no time to handle legitimate last minute emergencies, like your great buy.

Information sheets *can* get to the advertising department on time. We know. Some stores now fine departments whose information sheets are late. So much per day. Deducted from their advertising budget. It works. The sheets are rarely late. Obviously, it's a matter of priorities.

CHAPTER 4
GRAPHICS: WHAT THE AD DEPARTMENT
NEEDS FROM YOU

As we have said, *an ad starts with the merchandise.*

No matter how vivid your powers of description, and how hard you try, the best designed and illustrated ads come out of seeing the merchandise. The actual in-the-flesh goods.

You may have heard that we have "swipe" files . . . and we do. If you say "tuxedo sofa" or "striped shirt", we know what they look like. In general. But not your sofa or your shirt. Without the actual merchandise to work from, you'll get a fuzzy approximation of what you're selling.

So don't leave it to our imagination. We may be too imaginative! Or we may generalize so broadly we fail to communicate to the customer.

How about a manufacturer's photograph or drawing instead of merchandise? Not the same thing. The photograph's probably been retouched almost beyond recognition (did you ever buy a car that looked like a car in a TV commercial or magazine ad?). It doesn't inspire the way the actual merchandise does, merchandise we can see and touch and walk around.

If you're planning to use the manufacturer's photograph as actual artwork, there are other problems, too. It certainly won't be in your store's style. Try to imagine a page of 4 illustrations from 4 different manufacturers, each in a different style . . . and you're imagining a graphic nightmare.

It may not be right for newspaper reproduction. Most manufacturer's photographs are prepared for magazines or sales kits. And if it's in color, it probably won't reproduce well in a black-and-white version.

14

If it's a mat rather than a photograph, there's an additional problem. Newspapers using offset can't use mats. They must have glossy or reproduction proofs.

In any event, neither photograph nor mat is a good substitute for the real thing . . . the merchandise.

How about sending up "similar" merchandise to the advertising department? It depends on how you plan to use it.

If it's for the artist to draw from, just be careful. Very careful. If the only sample you can get from the manufacturer comes with long sleeves instead of short, tell us precisely how short. Elbow length, an inch above the elbow? If it will come in houndstooth instead of glen plaid or gingham instead of solid, tell us how big the pattern is. And so on. Spell out every difference in detail. Otherwise there's bound to be misinterpretation somewhere along the line.

On the other hand, if you're using a picture of similar merchandise from a magazine, a catalogue, or an art service as actual art work, think twice before you do. You may alienate customers. Even if you say that this is only similar. Because they'll come dashing in, only to find something other than what they ran in for.

It's not good advertising to show one thing and try to sell another. You'd boil if an artist tried to palm off an inaccurate version of your merchandise on you. Think of how the customer will feel.

So try to provide us with the actual merchandise, even if you have to exert yourself to get it. Even if you can only borrow it from a manufacturer for a couple of hours. Even if you have to play messenger yourself.

What else do we need?

We need specific instructions for art work

The ruffle around the comforter is the main selling point? Tell us . . . or we may show lots of quilted top and only a sliver of ruffle.

The cuffs are important? Tell us . . . and we won't pose the model with her arms behind her back.

The fullness of the skirt? We'll dramatize it. The back bow? We'll show a three-quarter view that includes the bow. A sweater for a swinging guy? Tell us . . . how are we to know it's not for a suburban mortgage-holder.

Your sample of a bookcase is mahogany finished, but the piece you're selling is blonde wood? It's easier to tell us at the beginning than to re-do the art. Get the idea?

Only you know all this. Don't keep it to yourself. Assume nothing. It won't do any good if it's in your head. Put it in writing. In detail.

Give us art instructions on a tag attached to merchandise

In most stores, copy is written first, then a layout is designed, then the finished artwork is done.

Your copywriter needs art instructions on the information sheet in order to tell the layout designer how many pieces of merchandise. Whether it's new art or old. How it should be shown.

But this information, plus specific instructions on where to put the emphasis, also belongs on a tag attached to the merchandise. So the layout designer can have it in front of him when he's looking at the merchandise. So the photo studio, if you use photographs, will have it. So the artist who is drawing it (and the artist may be a free-lancer who works at home, far from you *and* the advertising department) will have your instructions when he starts drawing.

If your store does not have a system that includes merchandise tags, institute one. You'll be a hero!

Want us to show merchandise in use? Then tell us how to use it

We need lots of background information when what something does is as important as what it is.

For example. A picture of an electric knife is an impersonal uninteresting object, selling nothing. An electric knife slicing a roast or a tomato immediately sells an idea to the reader . . . here's a substitute for clumsy slicing. Show the knife, of course. But show it in use as well, because use is what you're really selling.

Think about it for a moment, and you'll realize that lots of merchandise falls into this category. You don't buy a can of paint or a jar of hand cream, to take two extremes, for their containers. You buy it for what it does, and the product should be secondary to the action . . . and the words explaining the customer benefits.

This is true of almost everything that comes in a can, tube, jar, or vial. Yet our papers are full of giant pictures of aspirin bottles and jars of silver polish and cans of bubble bath.

Then there's the stuff that looks like nothing folded up. For example, all domestics. A pile of towels in full color is attractive. A pile of towels in black and white is a heap. You'll sell more towels if you suggest a nice setting. Or a tight close-up of a pattern or a border. Because you'll catch the eye of more readers.

A lace tablecloth just sitting on a table top will show every curlicue, but it will be a better illustration if there's a beautiful flower arrangement on the table.

The same is true of furniture and rugs. Room settings . . . human situations . . . are more effective because they pull the reader into the picture.

Tell it to us like it is . . . accurately

Your information and instructions should be correct as well as detailed. If it costs money to reset type, it costs even more money and time to change art or tear up a page and redesign it.

Because you told us the chair would come in velvet and damask . . . and we showed both. But you only want to promote the damask.

Because your best-selling china pattern, by far, is the plain white with a platinum rim and we featured the rose-bedecked, since you didn't tell us which was the more important.

Because you promised a vendor he would get the top half of the page . . . and neglected to inform us.

Because you didn't call us when the baby buntings turned up with a patterned hood instead of a plain.

We could go on, but we hope we've made our point.

Well, suppose there's been a misinterpretation. It doesn't matter whose. The time to make legitimate changes is when layout and copy are done. Not when the ad is in mechanical form and the artwork finished.

Once the type is set, the artwork done, and everything pasted up, it's going to cost you . . . your store . . . a mint.

You don't bother to look at layout and copy? Then, frankly, you're not doing your job. Insist on it.

You'll notice we said "legitimate changes". There is no right time . . . ever . . . for changes that are pure whim . . . and rarely for changes because you changed you mind.

Above all, avoid the worst sin: holding space until you make up your mind what to run. We've seen it happen too often. The buyer can't decide which skirt to advertise. So he sends up an information sheet on a pleated black flannel he happens to have in stock. We write the ad, design it, do the art. Then, when he gets the proof, he finally makes his decision: a belted tweed skirt. He crosses out the ad on proof, and starts from scratch. So do we. This is a sure way to make the ad department work against you instead of for you.

To make a dramatic ad, we need a simple story

That doesn't necessarily mean one piece of merchandise expensively sprawled across a whole page (although that's pretty good if you can swing it).

It means a minimum of also rans.

Ten items to a page, each with 2 or 3 line items tacked on, and 4 swatches on one. We can do it, but it won't be good advertising. Except for listings, clearances, and such.

6 styles of knit hats and scarves with 4 liners on other mittens and a small box on fur-lined gloves. All in a quarter page. The best way to plan a bad one.

We realize that you've already bought the mittens and gloves. They're in stock. But look at it this way. Suppose you had a choice between an exciting ad that would move mountains of knit hats and scarves . . . and an ad that would move some hats and scarves and a couple of pairs of mittens and gloves.

Is there any question which ad you would choose?

Especially if the exciting ad could generate enough traffiac in your department so you could sell the gloves and mittens anyway.

Don't get us wrong. We can do your ad either way. But we simply can't design an effective ad when we must include everything . . . even the kitchen sink. Unless we're doing a sink ad.

If you start thinking this way when you're in the market . . . in terms of what your ads will look like . . . you'll save yourself a lot agonizing decisions later on. And get great advertising.

We need a merchandise story that has graphic drama

Our function is to get your ad read. See Chapter 2.

Obviously, a dramatic ad will stop more readers than a placid one.

The simplest way to achieve this graphic drama is by having a feature on a page instead of dividing it into neat dull even squares. A feature is a focal point to catch the reader's eye. As we said, a simple device, but it always works.

You have 8 beautiful robes on a page. We can easily divide the page into 8ths, with 8 magnificent drawings. It will look nice, but will not be nearly as effective, as dramatic, as eye-catching, as featuring one robe big and giving the 7 others somewhat less space. We sometimes can't relate the ad to the proportions in which you bought merchandise.

If you try to plan your pages that way from the start, you'll end up with better advertising. Every time.

What if you have unrelated items on a page? The same is true. Try to make up pages where one item gets major space. So we can dramatize it.

You can also select merchandise with an eye for impact.

Certain colors photograph better than others. Ask your photographer which color to send up.

A very thin stripe, a tiny pattern won't show in a photograph. It will be a mass of grey. If the merchandise also comes in a bolder pattern, that's the one to illustrate. Elementary, but effective.

If a cable sweater and a plain sweater are moving equally fast on the floor, feature the cable sweater in your ad. For drama. So we can give you a luscious, tempting drawing or photograph.

So you'll stop more readers. Which is the other name for the game.

If a format is being used, stay within it

If you know that a specific store format will be used for your ad, merchandise to it.

That means if one figure is called for in your space, don't give us two. Or ask for two views of the same thing.

If the page is composed of long skinny modules, don't give us a 5-piece living room set. Give us an item, and save your set for another ad.

If the format calls for a single big price, don't give us 3 prices or a listing. Unless you tell us which price to feature.

In other words, don't ask us to do the impossible. Because it can't be done.

Do you really need art?

Are you asking for art because it's automatic? Or because you've heard that you can't sell it if you don't show it? Don't. Stop and ask yourself . . . would it be a stronger ad without art?

Let us give you an example, an ad that ran. And not from some little mama-and-papa store but one of the country's biggest chains.

It was a half-page in a tabloid size newspaper. A clearance of shoes for men, women, and children.

Two-thirds of the space was taken up by a drawing of heads: one man, one woman, one boy, one girl. Surrounded by "atmosphere" sketches of shoes: one man's, one woman's, one boy's, one girl's. Not specific merchandise because, we assume, there wasn't enough depth of stock in any one style to illustrate. Scrunched into the remaining third of the ad were a headline, 4 prices, 4 comparative quotes, and a description of the range of styles.

All in tiny mouse-size type because the art took up so much of the space. Yet it was only this third that did the real selling job. The art was meaningless.

A good strong all-type ad would have been far more effective.

Most merchants, unfortunately, never think in terms of all-type ads. "How will they know it's junior dresses if we don't show a junior in a dress?" is the usual cry. Have a little faith in words. Copy is a powerful selling tool. It answers all the reader's unspoken questions from what is it to does it come in my size to is it good value.

The all-type ad may be the most under-appreciated and under-used advertising technique around. Partly, at least, because everybody who's even heard the word advertising has heard that one picture is worth a thousand words. A maxim that's all myth, and we'd like to explode it for you. Here and now. And forever.

It's supposed to come from the ancient Chinese, many millenia ago. Well, think about it. Many millenia ago, 99% of the Chinese were illiterate. When your audience can't read, a picture is worth not a thousand words, but the whole dictionary! Our customers are not illiterate. Far from it. They're better educated and more sophisticated than any group has ever been. Any you still think you absolutely must have art in every ad?

Type, properly handled, can be your art work. It can stop the reader. It can be dramatic, intriguing, strong.

So don't ask for art when your stock is so broken that you can't illustrate the actual goods.

Use type for drama . . . and tell the story.

Nor should you request art unless a picture of your merchandise will add to, enhance, dramatize, create a mood, communicate, or otherwise improve your ad. If it doesn't, who needs it?

You ask for a nice room setting with a shag rug on the floor. Great! Then you also ask for 6 thumbnail photographs or sketches of carpeting to show your 6 other kinds of broadloom

The customer won't be able to see the difference between the dirty little blobs. Use the space to sell the difference in words. Don't waste it on art that just sits there, doing nothing for your ad.

When do we need merchandise and instructions for your ad?

On time. The same time you send up your information sheets.

We can't design an ad unless we have the merchandise and your art instructions. And the writer shouldn't put a word on paper without seeing it.

We can't create an ad in a vacuum and, as we have said several times over, the ad starts with the merchandise.

CHAPTER 5

WHAT THE ADVERTISING DEPARTMENT
DOES *NOT* WANT FROM YOU

It's a sad, but interesting, commentary that pros can always spot a store where the merchants are telling the advertising department how to do its job.

How can we tell? By ads that are not as good as they should be.

Which is why it's important for you to know when to keep your hands off, the "don'ts" as well as the "do's".

Don't lock the advertising in by making commitments to vendors that will result in weak ads

The best co-op ad is when only you and the vendor know it's vendor-paid. An ad that looks like your store, sounds like your store, talks to your customers in their language, to their interests.

In many stores these days, buyers cannot sign ad contracts with vendors until the contracts have been reviewed by the advertising manager. For store policy: some stores don't use manufacturers' logotypes. For impossible conditions: the vendor's name in the largest type on the page, or the vendor's ad always in the same position on the page, or a requirement to use vendor art and/or copy.

There may be fewer vendor-paid ads in these stores, but they're usually better ones.

The situation is understandable. Vendor money is tempting. So you promise them anything . . . and give them an ad that's bad for you and bad for them. Yet you'd be surprised how often vendors are willing to soften their demands. If you ask.

Here's where your advertising department can really help you. Get them to do a couple of good, exciting prototype ads each year and take them to vendors when you go ask for money.

It works. We know it does. We often show ads to audiences, ads that are not only magnificent but also produced tremendous business. After the audience has admired these ads, we drop our bombshell . . . vendor-paid. They're almost always ads that had been roughed out in advance and taken to vendors . . . and sold.

Of course, it won't work all the time, but you'd be amazed at how often it will. It's worth trying.

Otherwise you'll end up with something like this, copy from an ad that ran in a mid-west newspaper:

"Are Country Set girls spoiled? Who wouldn't be in separates smart as these that are easy-care, wrinkle-resistant, silky soft and shape-holding as well? It's all because they're of two-way texturized Sura-line®and ultressa®fabric woven of 100% Dacron®polyester by Klop-man Mills."

Except for art, headline, and captions, that's it.

What's wrong with it? Everything.

The writer tried. All the benefits are there, piled up in a long involved sentence that loses the reader. (And once you've lost her, she turns the page.) What in the world is two-way texturized? Who cares! The ad doesn't tell you why to buy the merchandise, or even to come see it. All it's really done is list the vendors, their pet phrases, and their trade marks.

You can almost use a slide rule and discover who's paying how much for what. Even the most skillful writer could not produce a good piece of copy with these requirements.

How does an ad like this get into print? Fear. And lack of understanding. When you get money from a vendor, you think he's really paying for that ad, don't you? And that if you don't do exactly what he asks, he'll take back his gold. Think again. The fact is that it's not *his* money that's paying for the ad, but actually *yours*. The cost of advertsing is built into the product. So stand up for your rights: how to spend what's really your own money on your own ads.

24

Don't ask us to do it like last year . . . or like store X

We don't do it like last year because the climate of buying as well as the merchandise changes each year. So do the subjects that are on people's minds, the phrases that will catch their eyes, the whole frame of reference to which they react.

There are exceptions to this, but they're almost all institutional. A & S has been running the same Merry Christmas ad for decades, Macy's used the same Thanksgiving Day Parade ad for 20 years. Some stores have an annual sale that's the major event of the year. Here, too, you can build a tradition because the appeal is fundamental . . . and because it happens only once a year.

Otherwise, an ad must be of today. So it must be a new ad.

We don't do our ads like Store X's for an excellent reason. We're store Y. With our own personality, our own customers.

There's nothing wrong with cribbing an idea, but it must be adapted to your store's style or it's a waste of advertising. This holds for graphics *and* copy.

To be sure, there are fashions in advertising and, as a result, lots of stores play "me-too". Look at your newspaper or, better yet, newspapers around the country. The moment one store sets a new style . . . a huge picture or wrap-around type or one-word headings . . . and it looks different and exciting, other stores play follow-the-leader.

What's wrong with this? The customer can't find your ad by skimming. She thinks it's some other store's ad and turns the page. The best ad for you is one that's immediately recognizable as *your* ad.

This doesn't mean a store's style shouldn't change. It should from time to time. But it should be a real change for the whole store, a fundamental change that reflects the direction in which the store is going . . . not a carbon copy of somebody else's success.

Don't ask for everything big

Where everything's big, nothing stands out. As W. S. Gilbert said "Where everybody is somebody, nobody is anybody". It's still true.

An ad needs a focal point. If you have six big pictures on a page, one of them should be big enough to be dramatic. Or the type. Something should grab the reader.

Too much bigness can be weakness. A big picture, a giant headline, and a huge price fight one another for attention. And the total ad loses the battle. Let one element dominate . . . and you win readership.

This is a fundamental rule of good design.

It's like having a tremendous breakfront, a towering chest, a ceiling-high bookcase, a grand piano, an oversize sofa and a 6-foot potted palm in one room. Nothing looks really big.

Don't tell us how to say it

Language is our prerogative, our area of expertise. Even if you've used your favorite phrases on your information sheet, don't expect the writer to pick up your language literally. Then the writer isn't doing his or her job.

If the copy says "a beautiful bounty of blouses" and you change it to "large assortment" because that's the way *you* would put it, you're not letting your writers earn their keep.

It's more than words. It's a way of thinking. The writer is the middle-man between you and the customer. You say to us "multicolored floral sheets" and what do we say? We say "Fall into a flowerbed to-night". We've added action, imagination, wit, and thereby involved the reader.

The exception to hands-off on words is the word of the moment for a particular piece of merchandise. If your writer says "open book-shelf" and you know that your customers are clamoring for etageres, tell the writer. The same if copy talks of elastic top pants and the magic selling phrase your customers are looking for is "Pull-on pants". (Who dreamed up that phrase is hard to say. Did you ever see pants you didn't pull on?)

Otherwise, stay out of the prose. Subconsciously, everyone considers himself a writer because he's learned how to read and write. Accept the fact that you are a merchant, not a writer.

26

Don't make decisions of art vs. photography on your own

That is, if there is a decision to make. Some stores use only drawings, some only photographs. If your store uses both, consult the advertising department.

Some things simply won't photograph well; they go muddy and gray. Tiny patterns, subtle textures (a cashmere sweater and an acrylic look alike in a photograph), the grain of wood, the lushness of a rug. Merchandise with small important details is better drawn: binoculars, silverware, intricate jewelry. Or merchandise that looks peculiar when photographed. Like shoes. Like sheer curtains.

Strangely enough, some luxury merchandise has more sales appeal when photographed because there's more realism. A superb photograph of a mink coat (but it must be superb) is more convincing than a drawing.

As a quick rule of thumb, anything where shape and silhouette and texture are interesting and exciting will photograph well.

Don't try to cram everything you own into an ad

We've discussed that in Chapter 4, but it can't be repeated too often.

If the advertising department says you'll have a better ad if they do a dramatic headline, one picture, and a listing for your 22 portable TV sets instead of the bunch of tiny illustrations you requested, listen to them. They're the experts.

If they say you're trying to get too much into an ad, listen to them. Then compromise, if necessary.

Just try to remember . . . they're not trying to leave things out so they can create an artistic masterpiece. They're trying to create the best possible ad to sell your goods.

Shall we give you an example? A buyer had scheduled a tabloid page with 4 patterns in ironstone dinnerware and 6 patterns in china. We discovered in talking to him that he really wanted to push the ironstone. He had a huge stock. The story was simple and good . . . a close-out at half price. He could deliver the ironstone (but not the china) in time for Christmas. But he thought maybe he could sell some china at the same time.

27

We unpersuaded him, developed a stunning ad for the ironstone . . .
which got a greater response than any other single ad he'd ever run.
It was a handsome ad, but the important thing was that the readers
could see the patterns, could grasp the story quickly, and understand
what they were getting for their money. All of which would have been
impossible with both the ironstone and the china on the page.

Don't ask for gimmicks

Like what? Like explosion shapes, exclamations morticed (cut into)
or superimposed on art. Whom are you kidding? Only yourself.

They're not readable. They say . . . ooh look at me, instead of the
merchandise. In a subtle way they pat you on the back instead of
telling the customers what you're doing for them.

The important thing is what you're selling, not your comments on
them. Which is what these gimmicks really are.

Don't ask to have the institutional "umbrella" on the other guy's page

You know full well that a major event or a store-wide sale will bring
the customers in. It will help sell your merchandise. But the big headline or editorial cuts into your space. Maybe even dominates your
page. Well, that's the way it should be. It's the news. The store, and
the store event, are more important than any individual ad. You're
not in business for yourself.

Don't make corrections, proof after proof

If you're lucky enough to get more than one proof from your newspaper, that is. Actually your corrections should be made on manuscript copy in most cases. When the proof of an ad reaches you, take
the time to go over it carefully. Look at the ad as a whole. Then check
the pictures, the prices, the colors, the way the artwork is keyed. Read
the copy. Do it yourself instead of handing it to an assistant. It's part
of your job.

If you have a good business reason for making a change . . . wrong
facts, wrong emphasis, a typographical error . . . make it. Once. Then
let it go.

There is no reason, and no time, for change upon change upon change. Or for tearing up ads and re-doing them on proof. Besides, we repeat, any major changes should have been made when you saw layout and copy. Remember?

You get a proof to make sure the facts are right. Not to make decisions you should have made weeks before. For full details on correcting proofs . . . wait till you get to Chapter 10.

Don't give us ancient pick-up dates for art or copy

If it ran 3 years ago, chances are we won't be able to find it, and we'll waste time looking. And don't give us pick-up dates for merchandise that is only vaguely similar. They do us no good. Or booklets that will be running next month.

This may sound elementary and logical, but you'd be surprised how often it happens.

Also information sheets so badly scrawled that the writer has to call for an interpretation. Most copywriters become handwriting experts after a while. Why? Because most merchants act as though the typewriter hadn't been invented. You don't have a secretary and you can't type? Then print.

Don't ask us to do the impossible

You put together a page of one pair of slippers, one garbage can, 4 pairs of kids' jeans, and a shower curtain. All equal space. All good merchandise at regular prices.

You want it on one page because we've told you that a full page has more impact than little ads scattered throughout the paper. Usually. In theory, you're right. But when there's absolutely no common denominator (not even a sale or other money-saving idea), you're going to end up with a weak page. If we tell you to break the ad into two ads . . . one for the soft goods, one for the hard goods . . . listen to us. We know when it's impossible to create an effective ad.

Don't keep asking us to do a couple of roughs for you

For a really major ad, for a campaign, for something you need to get vendor money . . . it may be important for you to show a few different treatments. But don't expect this for day-in day-out advertising. Why not? Time.

Most merchants think that the time-consuming part of creating a lay-out is noodling it up and making it look pretty. Not at all. The big time-consumer is solving the problem on paper. Making decisions. How many pictures? Should they be the same size? How much space should be for illustration, how much for copy? What will get the most readership? What kind of graphic treatment. What kind of art technique? Which type face? Etcetera. This all takes thinking . . . and time. Lots of time. Which we usually don't have. To do again and again and again on the same ad.

Don't tell us it's YOUR money when you don't like an ad

It's not your money, although it may be budgeted to your department. *It's the store's money.* We all work for the same store. You and us.

We're trying to do the best ads we can. If there's a difference of opinion, let's discuss it, let's compromise, let's try a completely other way of doing it. But tell us that it's *your* money and we'll probably get stubborn. After all, we're human, too.

CHAPTER 6
BE SOPHISTICATED

The advertising department is *not* always right. We make errors in judgement just as often as anyone else. If we're good, we make fewer ones, that's all. So beware. Learn to watch out for our little tricks.

Don't be taken in by the too cute headline

It may be too cute to sell. Like one in the N.Y. Times for swimwear: "Summer full of Sun-days". What does that say? That the sun will shine this summer? What's it got to do with the customer and her swimsuit?

The very very clever headline, or slogan, usually remembered long after the content of the ad is forgotten, is fine for a national manufacturer. But a store is not an Avis nor a General Foods. The ad problem . . . and purpose . . . are completely different.

The national manufacturer wants you to remember his name, and someday when you're in a store, any store, buy his product. It's important to him that you remember his ad.

A store wants you to come and get it . . . now . . . at this store.

This does not mean that retail headlines should be grim and dull. They should be bright and sparkling and light-hearted. But all this sparkle and wit must be based on merchandise and merchandise benefits. Not on irrelevant bon mots.

Be equally wary of the label headline

A label headline is just that. It sits there on the page, doing nothing for you except naming what you're selling. "Washer-dryer". "Magnavox stereo". "Sport jackets".

A headline should say or suggest what the merchandise does for *me*, the customer benefits we've been talking about.

31

It should have all the salesmanship that's used on the selling floor
. . . condensed into a few choice words.

Don't let the art department snow you with talk about white space

True, the eye needs some white space for relief, but it's the whole
space that counts. The total impression of the ad.

It's possible to fill a page wall-to-wall and have a great ad. It's a matter of skillful design, of the proportions between art and type and how
they're broken into interesting elements.

One of the most exciting and successful ads we worked on together,
so unusual that it became the basis for a whole campaign, had 5 pages
of typewritten copy. 5 pages!

Yet it was a fascinating ad, to look at, to read. Because the copy was
broken into a dozen different parts, each a different size, each with
a border. Some were illustrated, and a half dozen type faces were used.
And the page had a big dramatic headline.

Why was there so much copy? It took all that copy to tell the story
well. We were selling an abstract concept, the quality of meat in
Macy's meat department. You don't sell quality by saying "Quality
meats". You sell it by saying:

*"Did you know that only 10% of the beef raised in the U.S. gets the
coveted Prime stamp? And, of those, only about 2% are good enough
to make it to Macy's. Our major packer says he looks over 1900 cattle
to find 50 prime steer to fill a trailer for us".*

How do we know the ad was read? Buried somewhere in the middle
were a few sentences about calves' liver. The day the ad appeared,
we were sold out by noon!

Which brings us to our next point.

Watch out for copy that's self-indulgent

We're always being asked how long copy should be. There is no answer to that question.

Copy must be long enough to tell the story, give the facts, excite the
interest to buy, and urge the customer into the store.

Not a word longer . . . or shorter.

Good copy is a cliff-hanger. One sentence leads into the next. You can't stop reading it.

Unfortunately, not all copy is good copy. Some of it is typewriter patter, an ego trip. It fills the page with mood music, satisfying the writer rather than the demands of the merchandise and the customer.

How can you tell the difference? Read the copy with a customer's eye. If it keeps you interested and makes you want to buy . . . fine. If it loses you in a welter of words, then it's too long. But only then.

Make sure art is in proper relationship to copy

How much space for artwork, how much for copy? It depends. On whether you're selling a thing, an idea, or both. Or whether the item is dramatic and graphic. Or needs words to sell it.

Two things, however, must be avoided. First, the even-steven split between copy and art. It makes for a dull ad. Either art or copy (or type) should dominate.

The other is the big picture syndrome. A giant illustration, no matter what. A big picture when it's meaningful, of course. But when the words are more important than the illustration, then the type . . . the story . . . should be more important.

Beware of color that's used for it's own sake

Color should be used only when it dramatizes the merchandise and increases sales.

Before you spend money on color, ask yourself: will it help sell? Enough to justify the difference in cost? A stereo set on a brilliant yellow background will look more attractive. But will the use of the yellow background move more sets?

A pretty girl using a vacuum cleaner, all in full color, is certainly more eye-catching than it is in black and white. But look out. Your art department may give you an ad that's all girl (the decorative part of the ad) and a small vacuum cleaner (the dull object). And you're really not in the business of selling girls.

These may sound like extreme examples. But we've seen even worse. Color seems to bring out the "artist" in artists.

Make sure all merchandise that's obviously merchandise is priced

Even if it's only been put in as filler or background.

That doesn't mean the rug on the floor when you're selling a sofa. We can assume the customer will realize that your price is only for the sofa. But it does mean related merchandise. The drapery that looks naked on a window, so the artist adds a valance. If you don't price the valance in the ad, the customer will assume it comes with the drapery.

The dinette set that includes only the table and chairs, but you also show a china cabinet or bookcase.

Or, less obviously, what happened in this case, an ad for an umbrella table and umbrella. The artist drew in the umbrella stand which was *not* included in the price. Several customers demanded the stand . . . and got it . . . because the store was in the wrong.

Remember: if they can't read it, they can't buy it

If you get a proof with type so small, or so broken up in strange ways, or such a peculiar type face that it's hard to read, complain.

Our colleagues will probably hate us for telling you this . . . but there is no reason why headlines should contain hyphenated words. They look amateurish. If your ad has one, insist that it be changed. Either re-written or re-designed.

Avoid the numbers game when you're writing information sheets

A million dollars worth. A carload full. A not-too-experienced copywriter will grab at it as a ready-made headline.

It sounds so dramatic. And it is. From *your* point of view. However, from the customer's point of view, it's a clunk. I don't buy a million dollars worth of swimming pools. I buy one, and you've got to sell me on that one. On the other hand, if you said 18 different kinds of swimming pools, that's a number of another kind. A good number. Because it tells me that I have a choice.

34

While we're talking of numbers, we'd like to re-emphasize something. Too many merchants think that when they have a sale, the bigger the size of the price, the stronger the ad. Not so. You're not selling a price, but something at that price.

Accept the necessity for a store style, a store formula, a store format

The repeated impression a store makes in the papers is more important than your ad. So don't fight city hall.

You may think that your particular ad should be an exception. Perhaps it should. But suppose every merchant wanted to be the exception. Where would the store's style be? Down the drain.

If you seriously object to a format or a style, talk to the policy makers. Styles are not static. Formats are not forever. They are changed from time to time . . . for everybody. Maybe this is the time to consider a change. Approach the situation this way, instead of asking for exception after exception.

How do you handle real emergencies?

If the ad is in the works and the goods haven't arrived or the wrong merchandise was shipped, don't send your assistant with a message. Don't call the writer. Come yourself. Go right to the top, the advertising manager. Tell your whole story, straight and truthfully. You'll be surprised at how much sympathy and understanding and help you'll get.

If your record is good. If you don't do it too often.

Bring all the necessary material with you for the change in advertising: the merchandise and the information. Don't promise to send it later. Later is a dangling word.

If it's part of an ad that must be changed, substitute something that relates to the rest of the ad and makes advertising sense. Don't give us a dining room table for a page of mattresses. Don't give us a wall-sized home entertainment center for a page of small radios. The scale will be wrong.

If there's no time to do new art, try to pick up old art that's in character. Not a photograph for a page of drawings. If new keying is needed, do it yourself. On the spot.

What about the other kind of emergency, the hot buy you want to get into the paper as soon as possible?

The routine is the same . . . plus. See the advertising manager, bring your information with you, see the scheduling person, then talk to the creative people. Sit down with them and tell them your story. Get them as enthusiastic about it as you are. They'll work very fast . . . with the facts and your inspiration.

Again the same caveat: don't do it too often.

What if the ad is already released and at the newspaper and you must make a competitive price change?

Get hold of the advertising manager or the writer and see if they can catch the ad.

A buyer should NOT call the newspapers; they're not authorized to accept changes from anybody other than the advertising department. This is to protect you. So some competitor can't merrily call and raise *your* prices or change *your* ad.

If you're a sophisticated merchant, you won't think budget . . . but ad

What do we mean? If you're going to get a remarkable ad by changing the space or the medium, do it. Even if you have to juggle figures afterwards to come out even for the season. Be flexible within an ad. Great advertising was never created by slide rule.

Besides which, there are always budget amendments, aren't there?

Remember . . . there's no one right way to do anything

There are any number of good advertising solutions to any merchandise problem. Don't decide in advance how an ad should look or read. And, conversely, don't be satisfied with an ad that simply won't work.

If you have the right relationship with your advertising department, they'll try a different approach. Hopefully, one that will make you all happy.

CHAPTER 7
SALE ADVERTISING: MORE FOR YOUR MONEY

We have a confession to make. We suspect that many of the dreary sale ads you see are our fault. As advertising people, we don't consider sale ads creative, so we give them our second-best thinking. Plus the cheapest art we can get away with.

We're wrong, of course. In the average store, a large chunk of the annual volume depends on sales. Whether you like it or not, a good sale ad can bring in more business than your finest fashion ad, your newsiest idea ad. Faster, too. Naturally, you need both. If you don't run the fashion and idea ads, your sale ads will pull less and less.

Nevertheless, on the basis of volume alone, sale advertising deserves the best creative effort. Yours and the ad department's.

Any merchant or ad person who thinks that all it takes to do a good sale ad is to tack on the word "Sale" and make the price big has a lot to learn. Sale advertising takes special and different thinking than regular advertising. On the part of everybody.

More than any other kind of ad, a sale ad must be convincing, persuasive. It must make the merchandise sound desirable, the value irresistible. All without hype.

We've spelled out some of the generalities in earlier chapters. Now let's be specific.

Urgency

You want them lined up at your door tomorrow at dawn, don't you? We can, and should, make your sale ad look and sound urgent. You can help us.

A time limit on the event is a proven people-mover. "One Day Sale". "Three Days Only". "Last 2 days". "Prices go back up tomorrow". "Sale ends Tuesday". And every variation thereof.

But beware. Don't give them too long to make up their minds. "This month only" can actually be a deterrent to action. The shopper sees it, thinks . . . there's plenty of time. I don't have to rush. Then forgets. A week is about the maximum for urgency. A shorter time is even better.

If you have a limited quantity, by all means say so. It's another people-mover. Or the give the exact number. "Only 22" is great. Provided the number isn't too big. If you're the Giant Emporium, your limited quantity of 200 may, indeed, be a limited quantity for you. To the customer, it sounds like a lot. So much she may suspect you got stuck with them and they're not very good.

Note: In some states you have no choice; "limited quantity" is a forbidden phrase. In Connecticut, for example, the specific number of items must be stated when quantities are limited. This is to protect honest stores from unscrupulous bait advertisers.

Honesty

A sale ad must be even purer than regular advertising. It's more suspect in today's climate of consumer cynicism. So please don't feed the advertising department exaggerated claims, inflated comparatives, half-truths, or weasel phrases. We might use them. Then you'll be in trouble. With customers and even, perhaps, with the law.

Don't commit sins of omission either. If you have broken sizes, for example, say so. If you don't have all the colors listed in all sizes, say so. Or you'll disappoint or maybe enrage a lot of customers.

Look at it from the customer's point of view. (Always a good idea.) She's been searching for wine-colored boots. You run a boot sale. A good value, a good price. It sounds exactly like what she wants. And, hurrah, the ad says "In black, tobacco, and wine". She scrambles in. To find you have wine boots only in sizes 6½ and 10½. Neither of which she wears. She feels that you've fooled her. And you have.

It would have been so simple, and so honest, to say "not all colors in all sizes". Or "wine in 6½ and 10½ only". You wouldn't have raised her expectations. Instead of blaming you, she would have blamed her own bad luck. Quite a difference.

There's more to say on the subject, and we've said it. On pages 10 to 11, in case you missed them.

Value

This is what you're selling. What a sale is all about. You may be satisfied with a giant price, a stong comparative, and an ocean of black type. The customer isn't. At least, not usually. If you're selling bread at a penny a loaf or sheets at a buck, sure. But how often do you promote a communicable item like these?

Black type may stop the casual reader, but it's the message that counts. The words that convince her that this is a value worth investigating.

How do you get the idea of value across? We can do it for you; it's our job. But we need certain facts from you, facts that should be on every sale information sheet.

1.   The reason for your sale, if there is one. A manufacturer cut too many. A warm winter so you got stuck with woolies. A special purchase. The reasons are almost ad infinitum. And, as we have said, only *you* know them. The only possible exception is the event. The White Sale. The Storewide Sale. Baby Week., etc. These can be reason enough, although even these are improved when you provide real stories for individual sales within the event.

2.   Famous brand names. They're reassuring. They say quality. They say value. They give the customer confidence. They can be shopped and your prices compared.

3.   Merchandise information. Every fact that proves that this is, indeed, a lot for the money. Every customer benefit. Every superiority.

Let's assume you're sale-pricing a group of $599 tuxedo sofas at $499. How does the customer know they were worth $599 in the first place?

Telling her simply isn't enough. We must prove it to her. We must talk construction. We must talk fabrics. We must talk fashion. We must imply our reputation for fine furniture. We must persuade her, not bludgeon her.

Built-in events

We all tend to take the annual and perennial sales for granted. To a certain extent, we're justified. When you headline "Anniversary Sale" or "January Drug & Cosmetic Sales", years of conditioning (and millions of dollars of advertising) have led the customer to expect good buys. Extra drama, however, can be added by the way *you* plan and schedule such an event.

The problem is that most of these sales drag out too long. It's almost impossible to sustain excitement for a month or even 3 weeks. The sales under the banner grow dull and boring. To the customer.

How can planning help? Let's suppose you have an annual 3-week Storewide Spring Sale. Naturally, you start with a bang. A big blast. Then, instead of letting the sale drift and slowly die, plan a mini-event in the middle. Anything from your traditional green flag or red flower day or even assistant buyer's day. Or develop a new event which can turn into a tradition, by repeating it year after year. A spectacular with as much space and money behind it that you can afford. Even if you have to steal it from other ads you've planned during the sale. End with another blast. A count-down. Last 3 days. Last 2 days. Last day.

You'll bring back customers who shopped your sale when it began. You'll attract new customers who missed your grand opening. Or didn't bother to shop it.

Prices

"Sale! Every lamp half price!" sounds great. It *is* great. But what does it mean? ½ price of what? Unless you back it up with actual prices somewhere in the ad, it's basically meaningless. To that most important group of people: your non-customers. Who don't shop your store regularly, so have no notion of your price points.

40

Let's say you're Ms. M. You could use a new lamp and, in the back of your head, have decided you might spend about $50 on one. You look at the ½ price sale and you hesitate. After all, ½ price might mean as much as $100 for the least expensive lamp. So you turn the page.

Give prices. And do the arithmetic. ½ price, regularly 75.96, is certainly better than just ½ price. But, ½ price, now only 37.98, is clearer. People are lazy. They won't do the figuring. Besides which, some quick reader may assume that 75.96 is the sale price.

We're not suggesting that you pile up numbers. They don't all have to be in the heading. Merely that you understand how readers react.

Almost as bad as no price is the broad, non-specific price range. Sportswear, reg. $39 to $129, now $20 to $99. Again, it leaves customers without a clear idea of what they'll have to pay. It's smarter to break it up into groups at narrower price ranges. If the art department says they need the big prices, do the broad range, then a listing as well.

Whatever you do, if you cherish your reputation, keep your prices honest. "Up to 50% off" is a weasel, and you know it. "15% to 50% off" is more honest. Therefore more convincing. Provided, of course, that you have enough goods at 50% off to justify even mentioning it.

A few don'ts

Please don't insist that we name every little sale. Especially when you have at least one every week. You'll end up with Ground Hog Day Sale. And you'll deserve it!

We know several chains that run weekly newspaper inserts. Always sale. Always a name, a title. Not always good or natural. They actually weaken the impact of their genuine diamond-studded values this way.

There's nothing wrong with the word "SALE" and an explanation of either the reason behind the sale or what the sale means to the customer. The former is up to you. Fortunately you can leave the latter to us. Arm us with the facts and we'll come up with a good sentence or two. More persuasive than a phony sale name.

41

Don't go to the well too often, then blame us because each successive sale is less potent. And don't expect us to turn your dogs into overnight sensations. We're advertising people, even the best of us. Not fairy godmothers.

Don't add a zillion also-rans to each item. If an also-ran is important, it deserves space of its own. If it's not, why weaken your ad?

Don't insist on art when art isn't essential and does nothing for the ad, except cost money. We've heard it often. How will they know it's for men if we don't show a man? How will they know it's liquor if we don't show a bottle? They can read, can't they? Words will do the job very well.

Don't request atmosphere art. A suggestion of swimsuits or TV sets. Because you have no depth of stock. Or the maker won't let you show his merchandise. It's meaningless. Again, words will do a better job.

Don't ask us for an ad that's out of character with the store style or store personality. Sure, once in a while it's justified. Effective. But not often.

What to watch for in copy and design

Ideally, a sale ad should be simple, clean, direct, clear. The reader should get the message instantly. Then be persuaded that this is an opportunity too good to miss.

Copy shouldn't be too cute, although it can be light-hearted. It must talk value and not depend on the word sale alone.

Like any ad, it should be easy and inviting to read. If you have listings, type should be legible. If you have prices at the end of each listing, they should line up with leaders (dots . . .) so the reader doesn't have to use a ruler to find out which price goes with what. If there are lots of listings, the gray mass of type should be broken up with headings.

In all other ways, a sale ad should incorporate all the principles of good advertising. From customer benefits to graphic drama. Always selling value as well as merchandise.

CHAPTER 8

HOW TO SELECT MERCHANDISE FOR ADS

There are two faces to this problem, both equally important. One is general: how to select merchandise to advertise. The other is how to select it for a specific ad.

They're important because, as we said in Chapter 1, "Advertising does not start in the advertising department. It starts when you're in the market...buying".

So there you are. In the market. You know your store's merchandise objectives. You know your market and your customers. You know your open-to-buy and the gaps in your stock. You've read your trade journals and the fashion magazines. Then you buy. The merchandise arrives. If you're lucky, on time.

While you're buying, the advertising department has been planning the ad schedule. You're down for a number of ads and an advertising meeting has been scheduled.

What should you present for advertising? Of all the things you've bought, what should you choose?

We appreciate the problem. So much depends on your skill in picking the right goods at the right time for your market. Ultimately, it's up to you, but there are a few guidelines.

What to advertise ... in general

1. If it's been checking out on the floor and you can get more, advertise it.
2. If it's a communicable item at a good price, advertise it.
3. If it's a hot item at a regular price, advertise it.

4. If it's a staple at the right time, advertise it.
5. If it's new and news, advertise it.
6. If it's a sale, clearance, or special purchase, you have little choice. Advertise it.
7. If it was advertised and sold well, keep on advertising it.

What to avoid . . . in general

Don't select merchandise merely to fill space. You'd be better off saving your money till you have something worth running.

Don't advertise an item only because the vendor has offered to pay for the ad. Or part of it. If it meets any of the criteria above, sure, run it. If it doesn't think twice. If *you* were paying, would *you* advertise it?

Keep away from hunches. They may pay off once in a while, but the odds are against you. Play the winners. New fashions and new ideas, by the way, are *not* hunches. A store has to give the news. That's what customers expect of you. It's an investment in the future of your department and the store itself.

Don't try to get rid of your mistakes by continuing to advertise them. They will not do any better next week than they did last week. Except maybe in a clearance. There's very little that we, as advertising people, can do when customers shun an item.

How to select merchandise for a specific ad

To a great extent, this depends on the kind of ad you'll have. For the sake of simplicity, we're going to break the subject down into 5 parts, the 5 most commonly used ad forms.

There are dozens of variables and permutations. All acceptable. All depending on the creativity of the advertising department and you.

The one common denominator is a single idea. One idea at a time. No fillers. No also-rans. They confuse the issue and distract the reader.

For example. If you're advertising sheets, the common denominator could be all-flowered sheets or all solid colors or all famous names or an assortment at a single price. This gives the advertising department a positive story to work with. The result? A better ad.

If it's women's shoes, it could be all boots. Or a new heel height. Or even a variety of shoes with the common denominator suede. Or even a color.

With chairs, it could be all loungers. Or side chairs. Or all chrome. Or an assortment at one price.

We're sure you get the idea.

The individual or item ad

This can be as small as 1 column x 5 inches. Or as big as a full page. Depending on the importance of the item. And your budget.

The most popular size today, used by specialty stores and department store alike is 2 or 3 columns by 7 or 8 inches (200 or 300 lines). It can be used for a sale or non-sale goods.

The ideal merchandise for this type of ad is a single item. Possibly a collection of small items. like jewelry or cutlery. Always with a common denominator. Always a single story.

The classification or theme ad

This can be any size, up to a double truck. Since the objective is to show a variety of styles...variations on the theme, as it were...it's obvious that a reasonable amount of space is essential. Even if it's been decided to show only one or two pieces of merchandise and create an ad that's a stopper.

Most of these ads have at least 3 items in them. Although 4 or 5 can be used effectively, if there's enough space. Again, all with a single idea, a theme. Which is what you're selling. Don't try to advertise everthing you own in an ad like this. The 3 or 4 or 5 items should stand as symbols of the broad classification or idea.

All the merchandise can be shown same size or 1 or 2 dramatized and the others smaller. However, if only 3 are to be shown, don't ask for 2 big pieces and one small one. It doesn't work. They either have to be all same size or one large and the other 2 small for an effective ad.

The assortment ad

Here, the larger the space and the more merchandise, the better. 2 or 3 do not an assortment make!

Also, the narrower the category, the narrower the common denominator, the better the ad.

Here's an example of what we mean. Let's say you have a superiority in women's active sportswear. More jogging suits, golf skirts, tennis dresses, etc. You could plan an assortment ad that included all. Each group clearly defined. But, at best, you could only show a few in each group. Any store in your area would have that many in stock. An ad like this does *not* dramatize *your* assortment superiority.

Instead, make a decision. Do the entire ad on golf skirts. Show as many as you can.

The customer's reaction is inevitable. "If they have that many golf skirts, wow! They must have just what I want in other active sportswear".

Your writer, of course, says so in the ad. And you've dramatized your assortment superiority. Merchandise an ad so it's a stopper. Memorable. Making your point clearly.

Just be sure that the graphics are carefully handled to emphasize the merchandise differences. Especially when such differences are small. The best technique is all art the same size and in about the same position.

The omnibus ad

If you ask any designer, he'll tell you this is the most difficult kind of ad to do. Mostly because of the variety of unrelated merchandise and the variables in the individual units.

Each unit should be merchandised, depending on space allocated, as a single separate idea. However, since an omnibus is, basically, a compromise, you'll have to expect compromise from the designer.

His job is to make the entire omnibus a single effective ad. He may have to make your space a little bigger or a little smaller. He may ask for fewer items, or even more, to satisfy the over-all design.

The module, build-up or stack ad

This is the modern version of the omnibus ad. Each unit of advertising is an entity, standing on its own.

Each ad is merchandised as a single idea ad. Each ad contains its own store logotype.

Modules can be treated as single ads. Or stacked one on top of the other. Or used in combination; some stacked, some alongside others.

From the merchant's point of view, *your* point of view, the greatest asset of this technique is impact, the individual impact for each merchandise story. Because it's flexible, there are no compromises here.

It also solves the age-old problem. When you have 3 disparate items, are you better off with individual ads strewn throughout the paper, or with a major space ad including all of them? A briefcase, a toaster, and a robe make a pretty weak omnibus. Not to say messy. As a stack of 3 individual modules, it's a fine ad.

Note: All of the above is, as you realize, choosing merchandise for newspaper advertising. You'll find the criteria for broadcast when you reach those chapters.

CHAPTER 9
HOW TO FILL OUT AN INFORMATION SHEET

There is no ideal information sheet, pink sheet, blue sheet, advertising request, or whatever your store calls it.

Because each store is different and the requirements change within each store.

Right now, for example, many stores are charging for delivery on all items or not accepting COD's. Yet their advertising request sheets often do not yet provide for this information. Which means a last minute hassle to add these facts to an ad. (Information sheets, as well as advertising, can use up-dating from time to time.)

That's why our wrong-and-right information sheets that follow this page are not meant to be literal formats, but a guide to show you which facts the advertising department needs.

We have skipped the merchandising and statistical stuff that usually goes on such sheets. Like the retail value of goods, how many days on sale, how much vendor-paid, etc. We have also skipped spelling out the other media and confined this to newspapers only. Although the same information sheet, with the same facts, could probably be used for direct mail and, with minor changes, broadcast.

Suggestions:

Use one sheet for each item advertised, unless you have a listing. This provides your ad department with a clear story and eliminates confusion on whether the credenza or the table is walnut or mahogany.

If you can't have it typed, print.

Fill out everything, from top to bottom.

Don't try to write copy. Just give us the facts.

Don't be cryptic. Assume we know nothing. Mistakes are more likely to happen when you forget to tell us something.

There should be covering instructions on how to fill out an information sheet, either on the back of each sheet, or on the cardboard if the sheets are padded. As a constant reminder. And for the new kid on the block. Writing an information sheet for the first time.

DEPARTMENT MANAGER'S ADVERTISING REQUEST

#1. **NEWSPAPER** *Gazette* **SPACE** *1/2 pg* **DATE** *Sunday 9/7*

TYPE OF AD: (sale) best seller regular merchandise
institutional other...

#2. **ITEM** *Irregulars of quilted bedspreads and matching draperies*

#3.

STYLE #	PRICE	COMPARATIVE	QUOTE	SIZE	COLORS
92-F	*$49*	*reg.*	*$69*	*full*	*assorted*
92-Q	*$69*		*$89*	*queen*	*multicolor*
92-K	*$85*		*$100*	*king*	*florals*
92-D	*$29*		*$39*	*84"*	

#4. **MOST IMPORTANT CUSTOMER BENEFITS**
Most wanted bedspread

#5. **OTHER SELLING POINTS** (in order of importance)
Dress up your bedroom for Fall. Hand-outlined quilted to the floor for the fashion look in today's bedroom. Easy care.

#6. **MATERIAL OF WHICH MERCHANDISE IS MADE**
Dacron and cotton with polyester fill

#7. **OTHER SPECIFICATIONS**

#8. **HOW MANY ILLUSTRATIONS** (1) (B&W) COLOR
No. of old photos   no. of new photos
No. of old sketches   no. of new sketches (1)

Which item to be featured?

Which points to be emphasized?

If old art, date when ad last ran.   Attach proof.

#9. **MAIL ORDER** (Yes) No **PHONE ORDER** (Yes) No **COD** Yes No

SHIPPING CHARGES: in area   outside area

#10. **ON SALE AT**   main store   branch a   branch b   branch c

Compared to many information sheets we have seen, this one sample shown here is bursting with facts. But not enough of them. It assumes a lot of knowledge on the part of writer and designer, and skips important customer information. Let's take it point by point.

#2. The way this is written, it sounds as though the draperies are quilted. Which size and price should we feature?

#3. Comparative language for irregulars should be "if perfect", not "regularly." Otherwise you're comparing apples and oranges.

What is the actual size in inches of each spread? The customer wants to know.

What are assorted florals? The customer wants to know.

#4. "Most wanted" is great for you, but is it really the most important customer benefit?

#5. She knows it will dress up her bedroom. This does not answer all her other questions. What kind of corners? How is bottom finished? What kind of irregularities? Can it be washed by machine? And how about the draperies. Are they pinch-pleated? Lined?

#6. Dacron is a registered trademark, not a fiber. If you don't want DuPont and the FTC down on you, you'd better say Dacron® polyester.

#7. The facts you don't include in #5 belong here. All of them.

#8. Do you want to feature the bedspread and not show the draperies? Or do you want to show the draperies on a window behind the bed? You don't tell us. Or what you want emphasized. The quilting? The flowers? Should we show bottom?

#9. Fill out completely. Write "none" if there are no shipping charges.

#10. Fill out completely.

Now to see how the information sheet should have been written so the advertising department could create a good ad, turn this page. . . .

51

IMPROVED ADVERTISING REQUEST

#1. NEWSPAPER *Gazette*   **SPACE** *1/2 pg.*   **DATE** *Sunday 9/7*

    TYPE OF AD: (sale)   best seller   regular merchandise
    institutional   other ....

#2. ITEM *Irregulars of quilted bedspreads; matching unquilted draperies. Feature full size, list others.*

#3.

STYLE #	PRICE	COMPARATIVE	QUOTE	SIZE	COLORS
92-F (full)	$49	If Perfect	$69	96x110"	multicolor
92-Q (queen)	$69		$89	103x120"	flowers on
92-K (king)	$85		$100	120x120"	green, blue,
92-D (drapery)	$29		$39	48x84"	rose grounds

#4. MOST IMPORTANT CUSTOMER BENEFITS
Hand-outlined quilt to the floor. Machine wash-and-dry.

#5. OTHER SELLING POINTS (in order of importance)
Wanted fashion bedspread at low price. Rounded corners. Corded bottom. Dramatic floral print.
Unlined draperies in same fabric, pinch-pleated tops.

#6. MATERIAL OF WHICH MERCHANDISE IS MADE
Dacron®polyester and cotton with polyester fiberfill.

#7. OTHER SPECIFICATIONS
Tiny irregularities will not affect appearance or wear. Comes in queen and king as well as full size.

#8. HOW MANY ILLUSTRATIONS (1) (B&W) COLOR
No. of old photos   No. of new photos
No. of old sketches   No. of new sketches (1)

Which item to be featured? *Show bedspread with drapery on window behind it.*

Which points to be emphasized? *Quilting; show rounded corner and corded edge.*

If old art, date when ad last ran.   Attach proof.

#9. MAIL ORDER (Yes) No **PHONE ORDER** (Yes) No **COD** (Yes) No
SHIPPING CHARGES: in area *None*   outside area *1.50*

#10. ON SALE AT   main store ✓ branch a ✓ branch b ✓ branch c ✓

CHAPTER 10
HOW TO CORRECT PROOFS

Do you know what kind of proof system your store is on? If you don't, find out. It makes a lot of difference in how you make changes.

There are three basic systems.

1. Unlimited proofs

Your newspaper will give you proof after proof, if you need them. And take corrections on all of them. Thanks to paper shortages and labor costs, this system is fast disappearing.

Moreover, many papers charge for what they call AA's (author's alterations), copy changes . . . other than simple, normal ones like prices, colors, sizes. Other papers make a charge if more than 20% of the ad is revised. If your newspaper does this, you can run up quite a bill if you're change-happy. For which there is no need if, as we have repeatedly pointed out, your facts were right in the first place.

2. One-proof system

This means one set of corrections, then the ad is released to the newspaper. And that's it.

Your advertising department may possibly get an insertion proof, showing the way the ad will look in the paper, with all the changes made. Theoretically, you can't correct this proof. But if the ad hasn't gone to bed, a major error, like an incorrect price, often can be fixed. Or it can be caught in a later edition of the paper.

Most of the time, however, it's too late to do anything with an insertion proof except look at it.

All this may soon be academic. This system is also disappearing because of computer set type and camera-ready copy.

3. Manuscript OK system

Chances are that your newspapers are now setting type by computer and preparing what are called camera-ready mechanicals. These consist, very simply, of all graphic material and copy pasted into position exactly as the ad will appear in the newspaper. Everything. From headlines to copy to art to the little bugs at the bottom of the ad. It's then photographed.

More and more stores are preparing their own ads in the same way right in the store, then sending these camera-ready mechanicals to the newspaper. They have in-house production centers that turn out not only ads but also flyers, booklets, and all the other printed material a store needs. If your store has such a center, get to know it. You'll find it fascinating.

This combination of computer type and camera-ready mechanical means there are no real proofs. Which is why your advertising department must ask for all changes on manuscript, the original typed copy.

You're shown copy and layout and make all changes then and there. If any proofs come in (often there are none), you never see them. Only the advertising department.

In this kind of set-up, there are no second chances, no second thinking. You make corrections once, so they must be made carefully, accurately. Or else.

Let's all talk the same language

Typographers, proofreaders, and your store's production staff have a standard set of symbols they use for correcting manuscript copy and proofs. It's a sort of short-hand, a universal printer's language.

It will pay you to learn it and use it. Then there will be no mistaking your intentions.

Here are some of the most frequently used symbols and what they mean.

   _ℓ_ take out   ⁻/ hyphen

   ∧ insert at this point   ⁋ make paragraph

⊙ period		ⁿₒ¶	no paragraph
⅄ comma		stet	let it stand
⊙ colon		tr.	transpose
⅄ semicolon		caps	capitals
ⱽ apostrophe		l.c.	lower-case letter
⌐ space between words			

Please don't write between the lines

Like everything else, there's a right way and a wrong way to make corrections. The wrong way is to scribble between the lines or write long, elaborate notes.

The right way is to cross out the copy to be corrected. Draw a line out to the right side of the proof, make your correction, and circle it. Be accurate. Be neat. Remember, copy changes go through a lot of hands before appearing in the paper.

Here are some "how-to" examples of the right way to make changes.

Headline change

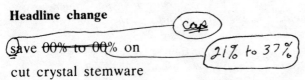

save ~~00% to 00%~~ on

cut crystal stemware

Note: never leave the arithmetic to the copywriter. And don't round off percentages. 21% sounds more convincing than 20%.

Price change

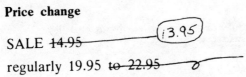

SALE ~~14.95~~

regularly 19.95 ~~to 22.95~~

Note: double-check your arithmetic. Make sure your sale price and your comparative quote really equal your percentage off if you use one.

55

Copy block change

(blue,)

A pride of pants and tops in solid brown, green,
or black. Machine washable and dryable, of course.
(Who irons these days?) The pull-on pants precisely
tailored in ~~polyester and wool~~; the shirt-sleeved *(60% wool, 40% Polyester)*
tops in a creamy ~~Kodol~~ polyester. Yours in S, M,
L, ~~XL.~~ *(Kodel®)*

*Note Corrections: line 1, a color added. Line 4, a correction of the
fiber content. Line 5, registered trademark must be indicated. Line
6, deletion of extra-large; doesn't come in this size.*

All of these changes, incidentally, would have been unnecessary if
you'd given the correct facts on your information sheet.

Changing listings

size	regularly	SALE
2x3	19.98	14.98
4x6	29.98	25.98
5x7	39.98	34.98
6x8	49.98	45.98

See copy A attached

*Note: If there are only a few changes, then it's OK to use the method
illustrated under "copy block change". However, if many changes are
involved (which wouldn't happen if your information sheet was accurate), cross out the entire block of copy. Retype or rewrite it and staple
it or paste it next to the copy block. If there's no room for this, attach
it to your proof and mark the proof "See copy A" (or B, C, etc., de-
panding on how many blocks are changed. We hope you never get
past A!)*

Spelling changes

Plaid sheets so pretty that you won't want to turn out the light. In a
smooth cotton-and-polyester ~~percalbe~~ by ~~Canon~~ that's . . . *(Cannon)* *(perca)*

*Note: be sure to double-check all spelling on proofs. Especially manu-
facturer's names, names of people (personal appearances, designers),
and names of imported products . . . like perfumes, wines, cheeses.
It's not a bad idea to get them right on your information sheet, too!*

Additional information

plus 75¢ for delivery

SALE 13.95, reg 18.95

Get this marvelous buy now. Come on the run . . . who
knows how long they'll last! *Sorry, no mail or phone*
4th floor, Main Store. Also at Brach A, ~~Branch B~~, Branch C

*Again, this is information which should have been on your information
sheet. Because it's omitted, an ad with no other changes must be sent
back for revise.*

Changing the way art and copy are keyed

After artwork is finished, it's obviously easier to transpose copy blocks
than to change the art. This is the way you handle it.

A. Blue, pink, white; sizes 12 to 18.   C.

B. Green, orange, mauve; sizes 10 to 16.   D.

C. Navy, blue, and aqua; sizes 10 to 16.   A.

D. Beige, brown, taupe; sizes 10 to 18.   B.

Transpose copy block to go A - B - C - D

*Note: When you're asked to key artwork, check the key letter carefully
against layout and final artwork. Never touch the artwork. Instead,
put the key letters on the layout (unless the ad is a complete mechanical
. . .then you put letters on a tissue overlay). If the proof is incorrectly
keyed, re-key copy blocks the way we've shown. Accurately. For this is
where more mistakes can happen more easily than in any other part of
the ad.*

Changing incorrect art on proof

incorrect art

*Note: If you checked your layout and OK'd your artwork before it was
sent to the paper, this shouldn't happen. But it does. Your assistant
may have approved the art, nobody may have been around to OK it, or
the art may have been finished so late you were long gone.*

Whatever the reason, here's the way to handle it:

1. X out the incorrect art on the proof . . . NOT on the original art.

2. Get to the art director or art department as fast as you can with the proof (or original art work) in your hand.

3. Have the correct merchandise brought to the art department immediately.

4. Either ask for the art to be fixed (if it can be . . . and we can add or subtract all kinds of things) or a new piece of art.

What if your changes don't appear in the paper?

Even if you made your corrections carefully and legible, slip-ups can still happen. DON'T call the newspaper. Go directly to your ad manager. Who will ask for the "book" . . . all the proofs, OK's, corrections. If you, the writer, and the production department made no errors . . . and the changes reached the paper in time to make them, it's the paper's fault. And you can ask for a free re-run. You may even get it. Depending on your paper . . . and its policies.

One last word

When you sign off a proof, sign it legibly or print. Initials are not enough. Add the date and your extension number. Then we'll know whom to call and where to get you if there's any problem.

Elementary advice? You'd be surprised how few buyers actually sign proofs this way. Which, as far as anybody in advertising is concerned, is the only right way.

CHAPTER 11

MARKETING

You're in marketing almost as much as your store's marketing or sales promotion director. Except that you call it merchandising. Which, in its broadest sense, is marketing, too.

As a merchant, you believe with the great Marshall Field in the basic marketing credo: Give the lady what she wants.

You buy merchandise to sell. Not always what *you* like. Nor what *you* might want to sell. But what your experience tells you that *your customers will buy*.

Suddenly the lady doesn't want what you've got to sell. And you begin to question your own judgement and experience. The change is rarely dramatic. It's more like a creeping paralysis. Gradual. Until one day your mark-down sheet or your P & L statement gives you the brutal facts.

Something is happening that's affected your department's business. (It's even possible that this may be happening throughout the whole store at the same time it's happening to your department.) You're faced with a problem. A marketing problem. What to buy? For whom? How do you reach them?

You're probably aware of the following factors that affect your business. But to what degree do they affect *you*?

- People changes
- Fashion changes
- Price line changes
- Competition changes
- Market changes

You cannot, in fact you should not, answer this on your own. Your solution is a meeting with your immediate supervisor (if he hasn't called you first) and the marketing or sales promotion director.

This will probably be the first of many such meetings before a complete merchandising, service, and sales promotion plan is developed for your department. A total marketing plan which will bring back the customers. In droves.

All the following aspects of your business should be analyzed:

1. A comprehensive merchandise review that includes price lines, fashion, assortments, timing, resources, etc.

2. A review of last year's sales promotion activities: media and media expense, proportion of sale to non-sale advertising, fashion advertising, assortment ads, advertised price lines. And, most importantly, the advertising effectiveness of your ads versus competitions'.

3. A review of your department: everything from housekeeping to the way stock looks. From lighting to fitting rooms to displays and signs. Even its location in the store and traffic patterns.

4. A review of sales services and sales clerks.

5. And, of course, your share of the market, your volume, and your profit statement.

This is the way a store can solve the problems of an individual department. But marketing is far broader. It affects and influences the whole store and all decisions in the store.

Retail marketing is based on the answers to six basic questions. Answers that every store should have. And update regularly. A profile of the store and its customers.

1. What is your market?
This is geographical. Is it local or wide-spread? Thinly populated or dense? Old neighborhoods or new ones or changing ones? A bedroom market, or do customers live and work in the community? Does it include developing areas? How long before the market will reach maximum saturation? What kinds of transportation are available, or being planned?

2. What is your position in the market?
This is your share of mind: your acceptance, your image, and your competitive posture. In other words, what do your customers think of you? The total store? Segments of the store? Who is your competition? What's your share of the market?

3. Who are your customers
Are they young? Old? Affluent? Middle income? Low income? Upwardly mobile? Way out? Middle of the road? Conservative? Transient? Male? Female? Both?

4. What do they need or want?
This is the heart of your business: your merchandise. Do they want the newest of fashion (both ready-to-wear and home furnishings)? Unique merchandise? Classics? Quality merchandise? Name brands? Bargains? What price ranges: high, medium, low? What services: sales people or self-service? Charge accounts? Delivery? Parking? What services do your competitors offer that you don't? What do you offer that they don't?

5. How do you reach your customers?
This is communications. Do you reach them through the newspaper? On radio? TV? By direct mail? Magazines? Billboards? Handbills? Telephone? A combination of some or all? In what proportion? How often? What does competition do?

6. How do you talk to them?
What do you say to them and how does it look? Black and bold? Light and lovely? Is it sale, sale, sale? Is it value? Is it selection or assortment? Is it ideas? A combination of some or all? What does competition look and sound like?

This is marketing, as we said, in the broadest sense. The kind of thing not enough stores sit down and do thoroughly. But when they do, the conclusions can affect *your* working relationship with the ad department. It won't be easy at first, but if the marketing conclusions are solid, they can result in improved business. For your department and the whole store. So we have some advice for you and the role you play in making the marketing plan work.

Don't be a die-hard media traditionalist. Sales promotion logic, based on the new marketing concept, may dictate a dramatic switch in media emphasis. Like taking dollars out of newspaper and putting them into radio. Sure, you tried radio once and it failed,so you're off radio. Or TV. Or direct mail. Or whatever. However, logic says it's right. At this time. For your market. Go along with that and give it your best. Be patient and give it a chance to work.

Don't merchandise ads the way you have in the past. A new marketing philosophy often calls for new sales promotion formats. New formats call for different ways to present your merchandise in layout, copy, and art. So be sure to merchandise to the new concept and formats. Results could be both surprising and profitable.

Reconsider your sales promotion timing. The new marketing philosophy may be based on greater fashion emphasis, a more promotional approach, or even a combination of both. Any of these may affect your advertising timing. Your ads may have to run earlier in the season. Or at the height of the season. Or in periodic bursts of saturation during the season. Discuss the timing for your departments with the ad department, so your ads can relate to the store's overall sales promotion philosophy.

Don't resist it: marketing is here to stay. More and more stores are appointing marketing directors who coordinate the efforts of the merchants and the advertising department. Which is the way it should be, because it's a total approach to the customer.

CHAPTER 12

FOR MORE PRODUCTIVE BOOKLETS, CATALOGUES, ETC.

Direct mail is a huge and varied subject. From a flimsy little bill enclosure to a 100-page or more Christmas catalogue to a postcard sent out by your sales people.

We are arbitrarily dividing the subject into two chapters. This one, on the big catalogue type mailings. And the next on the smaller pieces.

What they have in common is this: direct mail must earn its way. With postage up and paper up, it must work harder than ever to pay for itself. To bring in not only extra volume but extra profit as well. Otherwise it's a waste of everybody's energy.

How can you make direct mail more effective? By understanding its special problems and by working with your advertising department to solve them.

First of all, let us assure you that the same principles of good graphics and good copy that result in good newspaper advertising apply to direct mail as well. The whole bit. Consumer benefits, specific information, news, believability, simplicity, graphic drama, and so forth. Everything we've taken all these pages to tell you.

There is a great hidden advantage to direct mail. Once your customer has opened it, you have no competition. There are no distracting news stories alongside your ad, no other store touting *its* merchandise.

On the other hand, there are two serious problems. One is a long lead time, the months it takes to produce, print, address, and mail a catalogue. The other is limited space, the small page size.

Before we go into these, we'd like to tell you about a fascinating new development in direct mail.

The new look in catalogues

Many booklets are now being planned so that each page contains merchandise related either by use or by shopping patterns. The way people use things or buy them. This is thinking from the customer's point of view. Which always adds to productivity.

To give you two simple examples: instead of a half page of robes and, 6 pages later, a half page of slippers, the robes and slippers are being put together . . . even though they're from different merchandising divisions. Instead of page after page of pots and pans, each from a different maker . . . a page of coffee pots, a page of casseroles, a page of exotic cooking ware, like woks and paella pans.

The traditional way to merchandise catalogue pages in the past was by store division and vendor. Again, easy for you. But not much sense to the customer.

This may mean that you have to throw away the slide rule, selling a specific 1/16 or 1/8 of a page to a vendor. But it never was a good method for creating a booklet anyway.

Long lead time

It takes three or more months to prepare a catalogue and get it into the customer's letter box. This varies with the size of the mailing, the number of pages and how many of them are in color. An 18 page black-and-white booklet to 50,000 customers obviously takes a shorter time than 72 pages to 200,000 customers with half the pages in full color.

Let's take the three month figure. That means an August 15 deadline for the merchandise in a Christmas book that must be in your customers' hands by November 15.

It sounds unrealistic. It really is unrealistic. On August 15, you'll have to guess what your big Christmas sellers will be, before you've had any chance to see what's checking out.

Unfortunately, there's nothing you can do about it, except maybe be a good guesser. It's not that we're giving ourselves a lot of time. Get a direct mail schedule and study it.

There's surprisingly little fat in it. For anybody. Oh, maybe a day or so for possible emergencies, but that's all.

Our schedule is very tight. And a catalogue is a major job for the advertising department. Time is allocated for doing your art, your layout, your copy. Upset your part of the schedule and you upset the whole deal. That's why it's imperative that you have your merchandise samples and information on time. Especially for color pages which take forever to produce. That's why it's important that your merchandise and facts be right from the beginning. There's no time for big changes.

Once the booklet is planned and a "dummy" made, you can't pull out a page or even part of one. If you're early enough, before we've started to produce that page . . . you can substitute a similar item.

Once the booklet is in the works, however, it's extremely difficult even to substitute merchandise. No time.

As you have probably gathered, there is much less flexibility in a catalogue than in the newspaper. A color page, for example, once it's done cannot be changed. At all.

Knowing this, you'll only include merchandise in your booklet on which you have a firm commitment on delivery, well in advance of the on-sale date. Nothing looks sillier than a glowing picture of, say, four soup tureens with the statement "not available for 5 weeks" or "allow 5 weeks for delivery". They want it now.

This long lead time, of course, is one of the reasons why most booklets are dull. You have to play it safe with merchandise you know will sell, merchandise you know you'll have in stock. But that doesn't mean the copy and graphics can't be exciting!

Limited space

A page is a page is a page . . . or isn't it? A booklet page is a very small area. If you cram it, you leave us no space to sell the goods. To give customers the facts they need to make a buying decision. To order by mail or phone. Let alone inspire them to buy.

Maybe you think that if you have more things on a page, you may get a bigger return. In theory, you're right. In fact, you're wrong. Every item that you add, beyond a comfortable number, will weaken everything else on the page.

What's a comfortable number? It varies with the merchandise. Socks don't need much description. Mattresses do.

What you have going for you is the fact that a booklet doesn't need big page headlines, doesn't need out-size type, doesn't need really giant illustrations. Remember . . . there's no competition from other advertising, as there is in your newspaper.

You *can* get more into the same space than you would in a newspaper ad but, as we've said, there's a limit.

Also-rans, unillustrated, should be eliminated. They don't pull enough to justify cutting into the already small area we have in which to sell the illustrated goods.

If you have a long list of sizes (rugs, curtains, domestics), be sensible. Don't expect us to squeeze them into a square inch.

Don't ask us to show back views, fabric swatches, close-up details . . . unless you leave us the room in which to do them. Ask yourself: do you really need them? If you do, plan for them when scheduling your space.

Don't give us merchandise that requires long complex explanations, again unless they're scheduled with enough space for such explanations.

It's poor judgement to put an elaborate stereo or refrigerator-freezer with lots of specifications into 1/16 of a page. We can't say enough about them to communicate to the reader.

Editing facts

Amost all direct mail is designed before it's written.

This stems from the limited space available.

The writer works from the layout and counts every word. So every word must count.

Edit the facts you put on your information sheet carefully. The major customer benefits. The significant facts. The unusual facts.

If you have a group of similar items, tell us what makes one different from the next. So we, in turn, can tell the reader. A line-up of blenders that all look alike. A line-up of pantyhose. A line-up of white shirts. A line-up of shag broadloom.

Why should the customer pay 14.95 a square yard for the broadloom in the lower left hand corner when she can buy the broadloom at the top for 7.95? Not because you say it's better, but because you *prove* it's better. In words.

Asterisks, daggers, parentheses, and other dodges

Beware. In some states, it's illegal to bury certain information, much as you'd like to.

Consult your legal eagles before you asterisk an "irregular" instead of putting it in the headline. Before you dagger delivery charges. Before you add a parenthetic postscript in small type at the bottom of your page revealing that this bookcase comes knocked-down . . . or is available only at 2 of your 22 stores in all colors.

Nor does it make good advertising sense to bug up your page with asterisks, daggers, and such. First of all, you distract the reader. An asterisk in the middle of a headline will send the reader looking for what it means. And maybe never get back to the top of the page again.

There is even a school of thought that says (and can prove) that when you isolate facts, you make them even more prominent than when you put them into the copy!

The only justifiable use of the asterisk and/or dagger is when it saves considerable repetition and, therefore, precious space.

If every asterisked item is shipped by express . . . and you explain that at the bottom of the page or double-truck (*shipped express collect; see page 60). If every daggered item is only at the main store († at main store only) and, again, it's spelled out on every page or truck.

In other words, generalities that apply to several pieces of merchandise but are not actual merchandise information.

More mail and phone orders

Sometimes when we look at catalogues, we wonder how people can order from them. They must want the goods pretty badly!

We rarely see coupons that leave adequate space for the information the store needs (name, address, etc.) or for listing and describing merchandise.

Shipping information is usually in minute type and so garbled that it's difficult to understand.

Copy often fails to give the basic information the customer must have in order to know what's coming.

This is not true of the big mail order houses, the Sears and the Wards. Their mail order pages and instructions are models of clarity. No wonder they've been so successful.

There's little you can do about coupons and shipping information except constantly point out their inadequacy, if they are inadequate. And take the matter up with the advertising manager.

However, there's lots you can do about copy and keying.

Mail order copy

If copy *should* be specific in newspaper ads, it *must* be specific in a catalogue. Yes, your customer can come in and look at it or try it on, but you do want mail order business, don't you?

Nobody can order "assorted colors" or "misses' sizes" or "regulars, shorts, longs". How big is a "jumbo" salad bowl? A "king" size chair?

Certain basic information belongs in every copy block:

The major customer benefit: the why to buy
What it's made of
What sizes (fashion)
How big (home furnishings); exact dimensions
Colors and/or patterns and/or textures
Washable, drip-dryable, if it is
Knocked-down, if it is
A style number of some sort for ordering
Price.

The only source of this information is you. Once you give it to us, we'll add the embroidery, the sell. But we must start with the elementary facts that make it possible for a customer, sitting with pen in hand or at a phone, to visualize the merchandise.

If your booklet does not include these basic facts, you'll either get few mail or phone orders . . . or lots of returns.

And don't guess. If you don't have the facts, get them from the manufacturer. Tell him you're putting it in print, so *he* won't guess.

This does not mean merely attaching a specification sheet to your advertising request, unless you circle the most important facts. There are few things as maddening to a writer as being given a spec sheet with a dozen paragraphs, and then be expected to dig out the facts that will make a readable, sensible paragraph that sells . . . in exactly 30 words.

Some merchants, as a way of hedging, routinely ask for the statement "Give second color choice" on practically everything. Even when there are only two colors!

This makes life easy for you, but it discourages the customer. If I want blue gloves to go with my blue coat, I don't want brown. At any price. Or if my bathroom is all gold, I don't want green towels.

Use this statement only when there is a large range of colors and quantities in each are genuinely limited.

Keying

Some stores get cutesy with keying. Clockwise. From top to bottom. From left to right. It's OK if it's absolutely clear. But where does clockwise start?

If I'm interested in the third item from the left, must I wade through the other two captions . . . and count on my fingers to make sure I have the right one?

This sort of keying is particularly hazardous when you have a group of similar merchandise. A page of blouses. Plain sheets. And the like. Some dumb bunny will invariably count incorrectly and order the wrong thing. Then return it.

The impossible ideal is copy with each illustration. Impossible and very dull. The safest alternative is to key art and key copy with letters or numbers. It's not as pretty as leaving off key letters and using some other device, but it makes ordering easier.

It is your job to make sure the keying is accurate, to see the mechanical (the pasted-up art and copy) and check it. Don't wait till you get a proof. That may be too late.

Vendor-paid pages

One of the reasons why so few catalogues have any personality . . . too many are almost interchangeable . . . is the predominance of vendor-paid items in most mailings.

Unfortunately, most vendor money is behind the least desirable merchandise. We don't have to tell you that. The kind of stuff that would have a very low priority for your catalogue if it didn't come with a nice fat kitty.

What kind of impression do you think this makes on your customers? Month after month, year after year?

The solution is not to kiss the vendor money goodbye. It's too sweet for that. Instead, use the vendor money as a backbone, then spend your own money to add the interesting wanted merchandise that you'd put in a catalogue if you had your own choice. Merchandise that reflects your store, your personality, your customer.

Then go one step further. If you can.

Don't ask your advertising department to use vendor art and, certainly, not vendor copy. Treat the merchandise like any other goods. Let the advertising department interpret it.

You'll get a better return, not only for the vendor items, but for the whole booklet.

To think about

1. Mailings to your own list are usually productive. After all, you're talking to your own customers, who know you and shop you. But its strength is also its weakness. If you're talking *only* to your own cus-

70

tomers, you can't possibly make any new ones. This is not the route to go when you want to reach out to a broader audience.

The best method of increasing your base is to increase the size of your list. One obvious way is to get the names and addresses of cash customers and add them to your mailing list of account customers. The other way is to buy lists. Or borrow them. They're available. Ask your advertising department to check this.

2.   The computer, as you surely know, has made the difficult simple. It's now possible to get a lot more from your own customer lists quite easily. By cannibalizing such lists, as it were. Planning a lingerie mailing? Instead of sending it to everyone, the computer will burst out the names of customers who buy lingerie in your store, and you can send it only to them. Saving the printing and postage costs of a broad mailing. Reaching those who are the best possible potential prospects (but, as we again remind you, not making or reaching any new customers). The variations are infinite. Junior sportswear only to those who shop the junior department. A rug mailing to rug customers and your fur and fine jewelry customers, too. Or even a mattress or refrigerator mailing (or any major item with a long life) that eliminates anyone who's bought such an item recently.

Who says you can't use computers creatively!

CHAPTER 13
THE OTHER MAILINGS

This covers a multitude of small pieces. Too often, sins. Against every principle of good advertising.

Let's start with the simplest, certainly the one you can do the least about.

Bill enclosures

A bill weighs only a fraction of an ounce. A long time ago, someone asked himself . . . why pay postage for a full ounce and not use it? That's how the bill enclosure or stuffer was born.

Since then, every manufacturer worthy of his trademark, has been offering canned enclosures, printed in full color, ready to go.

They compete for the privilege of being included with your bills. Why shouldn't they? In effect, you are lending them your customer list, to expose their logotypes, their story, their merchandise.

What's more, a bill is not junk mail. It's always opened and looked at. Your booklets may be tossed into the trash basket unread, your one-day sale flyer may not rate a second glance, but an account bill is recognized as such and opened.

In our part of the business, these bill stuffers are called "store-name-goes-here" advertising. For a sound reason. The only part of the enclosure over which you have any control is the part with your logotype, coupon, and the shipping instructions. The manufacturer will print that page, too, but from the information you supply.

Stores welcome these stuffers. They can't afford to do such elaborate pieces on their own. But you can be selective about whose enclosure you'll use. As we said, you're offering the manufacturer a privilege. So be sure the enclosure does at least as much for you as it does for him.

Normally you request space (or should it properly be described as weight?) for an enclosure for a specific month from the advertising department. The direct mail manager, if you have one. You will be asked for a sample, so everything can be weighed together to make sure that the mailing doesn't exceed an ounce.

At this point, it's a good idea to consult the advertising department about the enclosure itself. Before you're really committed.

They'll check it for store policy.

Does it give a guarantee you can't honor?

Does it make a competitive statement that denigrates other merchandise you carry?

Does it violate your rules on pricing and comparatives?

Does it include anything that, in your locality, is illegal?

Plus all the other little nightmares that the advertising department is constantly on the watch for.

If the enclosure passes the policy test, the advertising department will provide you with the correct logotype to send to the manufacturer, the necessary mail and phone information, the tax and delivery information, the phone numbers, etc. Or they'll send it themselves, depending on how your store operates. Then you should see proof before the enclosure is printed.

Footnote

We don't want to open a Pandora's box. But. We all tend to take freebies casually. Even if the enclosure doesn't cost you a cent, hopefully your customers will respond to it. Not only by mail and phone, but in person as well. So have the merchandise on the floor where customers can find it easily. Properly signed. In a full assortment of the colors and sizes described in the enclosure. If you spelled out branch stores in the enclosure . . . this goes for them as well. Naturally.

Vendor mailings

This is a relatively new development in direct mail.

A manufacturer will come to you with a special offer, just for your mailing list of account customers. A roll-about cart with a TV set, 6 extra teaspoons with a stainless steel service for 8, a bonus gift for a purchase of cosmetics.

The literature is all prepared, usually quite elaborate with good-looking art and miles of words, on the successful Book of the Month Club formula. The merchandise can only be purchased by mail; often the coupon goes directly to a post office box owned by the manufacturer.

Again, in a sense, like the bill stuffer, you are lending your mailing list to a manufacturer. And the same caveats hold. Let the advertising department read it carefully. For facts. For competitive statements. For accuracy. For policy.

We have discovered, frankly much to our surprise, that small language changes can often be made in these mailers. Provided the change is not on a piece of artwork or in color.

Certainly it doesn't hurt to ask.

An even newer form of vendor mailing is the computer letter. As you probably know, this is addressed to the customer personally, with the customer's name mentioned 3 or so times in the body of the letter. And sometimes the customer's address as well.

Just one warning here, in addition to all the others. Make sure the merchandise being offered is suitable for everybody . . . we repeat, everybody . . . on your list. Or else you'll be giving some of your customers a good laugh.

A friend of ours who lives in a high rise apartment house in the heart of New York City, surrounded by concrete and asphalt, once got a mailing for an electric lawn mower. She would have shrugged off an ordinary mailing, but this was a computer letter. It ended with "and it will be a miracle to see how easily your grass is cut on 51st Street, Mrs. Jones." A miracle indeed!

74

Departmental letters and cards

Only one piece of advice. Don't write them yourself. Let your copy-writer do them. You may have majored in English, and your mother may still have every letter you've written since you left for camp at age 7, but you're not a professional writer.

Most letters written by non-writers are clumsy, involved, and far from clear. And usually too long.

Of course, you may be the exception. But don't bank on it. Get a pro to do your letter or card. Or write it yourself first, to get your ideas down on paper, then let the pro re-write it.

Trick: The use of "I" in a letter or card gives it a personal, warm touch that makes your message more convincing. Don't be afraid to use the first person. "I consider this one of the best values we've ever offered" is miles more convincing than "one of our best values". Psychologically, "I urge you not to miss this sale" is a greater spur to action than "don't miss this sale".

Have a signature on the letter or card. Your name. Somebody else's name. Even a fictitious name. A person's name . . . not the store name. It creates the one-to-one relationship that makes people read.

Private sales, shopper's specials

This is the sale offering. Either exclusively to your customer list. Or advance notice to them before you advertise the sale to the public. It takes many forms, but the principles are the same.

The secret here is more the way you merchandise the event than the way we advertise it.

We can make dumb merchandise at dumb prices look dramatic, but it won't fool the customer. Not for one minute. Big headlines and big prices won't help either. As we have said before, bigger is not necessarily better.

What you must have are communicable items at good competitive prices. Lower than the prices in your everyday advertising. Things people recognize as extraordinary buys. As soon as they see them. National brands. The season's wanted items. The good solid staples.

Give your advertising department this ammunition and then . . . and only then . . . your mailer can be a winner.

There are 2 effective devices to use in private sale mailers.

1. Make it sound private . . . just for you and our other good customers. How do you do this? A sale after-hours is ideal. There's no question it's special. Open from dawn to dark? Then go the route of telling them that only they know about this sale in advance. So they can decide now what they want and shop more efficiently, and get in on limited quantities. You can strengthen this . . . which brings us to No. 2.

2. Add a gimmick. Something you're offering them or doing for them that you're not doing for the general public.

Include an item in the mailer that only they can buy, if they bring the mailer with them.

Include a pair of tickets or a coupon that entitles them to a special extra discount on one or more of the items.

Offer to measure their rooms for broadloom before the sale starts, so they can know exactly how much carpeting they require when they come in.

Offer to put aside a fur coat in advance, if they call and tell you what they're interested in.

Gimmicks are infinite in variety. They range from contests, with the entry blank in the mailing, to be dropped in the store, to a free cup of coffee to a special activity for their kids so they can shop unencumbered.

A small furniture store in a small city invited its charge account customers to shop its 50th anniversary sale the day before the advertising broke in the newspapers. They used a plain post card. And added a p.s. also inviting them to stop by for a glass of champagne in the

76

merchandise manager's office. Result? Business almost doubled over the previous year's preview of the anniversary sale!

The idea originated in the advertising department. Where the crucial question was raised. Why should people rush in to shop at the preview when they know, from past experience, that they have a whole month to shop this sale? Obviously, they answered the question well.

Next time you want a gimmick for a special mailing, see what your advertising department can come up with.

Just remember, a gimmick is no substitute for good merchandising. Or good advertising.

You really don't need a gimmick, if your merchandise and prices are right. But it often gives you plus business on a day when you have big figures to meet.

Warning

Don't go to the well too often. Bombard your customers with private deals every month and you'll soon discover that you've reached the point of diminishing return. The less frequently you do it, the more special the private sale becomes.

Postscript

It is probably apparent that we believe everything in writing that comes out of a store should be written by writers. That's what you hired them for! Not just ads and commercials and direct mail and sale letters, but literally everything. Writers should review and rewrite, if necessary, form letters used to answer customer complaints, they should do account solicitation literature, help-wanted ads, handbills . . . anything that goes into print or meets the customer's eye. For a more professional job.

CHAPTER 14

SIGNS

Window signs

Our paragraph on writing window signs is going to be brief, because our message is brief. Don't. Let the advertising experts do them. Not the display people, but advertising. Why? Think of the window sign as another advertising medium. Which it is.

Hint: If your store thinks it's too commercial to include prices in the window signs, ask for separate prices next to each piece of merchandise. Passers-by want to know how much it costs. Especially these days. Even Bergdorf Goodman is doing it.

Interior signs

Chances are that you write them. That's what our informal research shows for most stores.

It's a very simple art. Be terse, be factual, be informative, be direct. A sign is read at a glance. It's not an ad. The fewer words, the better. If you can keep them under a dozen, great!

Cut back on adjectives. Cut out the obvious that can be seen (the merchandise will be right there). Cut down the flights of fancy, the long explanations. If the merchandise needs a lot of explanation, that's the sales clerk's job. A sign is no place to tell people how to use something. Merely what it is.

Provide only the facts the customer should know, the facts that will stop the customer.

And, above all, stay away from labels. They're uninformative.

Don't say "Men's Shirts, $15". Say something about the shirts. "Drip-dry shirts, $15". "Knit shirts", "Tapered shirts". If they're folded up, "Long-sleeved shirts".

If you have several facts, use bullets to list those facts in the fewest possible words.

40-piece

ironstone set

39.99

- service for 8
- ovenproof
- dishwasher safe

In short: skip the obvious, everything that can be seen, and stick to the plain unvarnished facts. And don't write complete sentences; they use too many words.

A special plea

Some stores consider signs ugly. They spoil the landscape. Could be. But you're not selling landscape, you're selling goods. Advertising is only part of the process. When customers respond to an ad and come into the store, we must make it easy for them to find what they're looking for. And, by proper signing, reinforce the ad impression. Signs can be so designed and written that they're both appealing and informative. If your store is eliminating a lot of signs because they look crass and inelegant, well, so are cash registers!

CHAPTER 15

BROADCAST: RADIO

What is a good retail radio ad?

What it is *not* is a newspaper ad read over the air. The requirements are different, from merchandising the commercial to the way language is used.

Nor is a good retail radio ad a variation on a manufacturer's network commercial. What's good for General Motors is not good for your store. Ever.

Then what is it? A good retail radio ad is a good ad, as we've defined good advertising in Chapter 2 . . . plus.

Plus characteristics inherent in the medium.

The main one is that they can't see what you're selling. Which requires you to think differently when you select your merchandise and when you write your information sheet. We'll go into that further on.

Another is that radio has urgency and immediacy built into it. This works for you. What you put on the air becomes news.

And still another is that radio is a selective medium You can pinpoint an audience. You can pinpoint merchandise to a particular group of people, if you wish.

You can also be topical in a way no other medium allows. As a matter of fact, you not only can be topical, you should be.

While a normal schedule should allow 2 to 3 weeks lead time so that every commercial is not a crisis, when a crisis does develop you can move faster on radio than any other medium. If it's live, with the station announcer reading it, all you have to do is supply a new script. That means a day or, in some cases, a couple of hours.

If your big sale is stormed out, you can be on the air the next day telling your audience that the sale's been extended. If pants are scheduled for Tuesday and your Sunday phone board sells them out, you can substitute another item. If a big news event happens in your town, you can change your commercial to latch on to it.

However, don't abuse this privilege. Or you'll lose friends and allies right and left.

Scheduling

You may be the one who decides whether a newspaper ad goes into the Daily Gazette or the Tatler, but radio is a much more sophisticated and complicated business.

You should leave radio scheduling to the experts, either your own experts, or the station's. There are pounds of demographic and psychographic material for every moment of every hour of every radio station. This is not hyperbole. A station knows, precisely, who listens to the golden oldies, who turns in to the evening news, who's glued to a pop star.

Let the experts pick your time slots. If you want the widest possible coverage, they'll work out a schedule that gives it to you. If you're zeroing in on a narrow audience, they'll find that market for you.

Warning: Don't expect a half dozen half minute spots spread out over a week to do a job for you. If that's all your budget can afford, either run them all on one day, or save your money or put it into your newspaper kitty.

Interesting arithmetic: 1+1 does not always add up to 2. If you use a combination of newspaper and radio for an item or an event, you can expect a response 2-1/2 times that of each one used alone. Always assuming that you are using both newspaper and radio properly. This is not a media manager's sales pitch, but a proven fact. In store after store.

The commercial: what we need from you

We need merchandise that can be described vividly in a few words. Remember, there are no pictures. This is what we call a communicable item. If you were selling eggs, there'd be no problem. Everybody knows what an egg looks like. But if you have a three-piece pants suit with each part in a different fabric in a different pattern . . . forget it. It's too complex for purely aural comprehension. It needs a picture.

If you have a plastic swimming pool in 6 sizes, each with slightly different specifications, promote one. Or you'll drown the listeners in a confusion of words.

We need a simple, clean story. Remember, there are no printed words, so the customer can't go back to the beginning to see what you're talking about. The ear is less attentive than the eye. You must pay attention when you read, but you can listen with one ear.

This eliminates also-rans. There is just no way to handle also-rans on radio. Asking us to include also-rans is like asking us to show color swatches on black-white-page. Sure, it can be done. Dark brown and light gray will have different values even in black-and-white. But it's not good.

We need a limited number of prices and percentages. A lot of numbers confuse the listener.

The worst possible kind of commercial is a laundry list of items and prices. It's a complete waste of air time.

Price ranges tend to be meaningless when they're heard rather than seen. Especially if there's a wide range. Like $10 to $50. You're not answering the question . . . what will it cost me? In the newspaper, we assume, you'd clarify the range by also showing single items at single prices.

We need specific details, as specific as radio itself. Just listen. Radio doesn't tell you that Joe Doe is a great ball player. They give his batting average. Radio doesn't give you a general "it will be warm tomorrow" forecast. They say the temperature will be in the high 80's.

Your commercial should be equally specific. And it will be specific only if you provide the advertising department with specific facts.

When words are few, there's a tendency to indulge in generalities. It's certainly briefer to say "every style of table" than to say "traditional, provincial, modern, and colonial tables". But "every style of table" is a waste of four words. It says nothing. In no way does it help paint a word picture for the listener. Which is what every commercial must do. A word picture is built out of specific facts. Word by word. Fact by fact.

We need examples to prove how good or how big an event is. "Our biggest sale in 32 years" promises a lot. It promises more if you add "everything from jewelry at half price to giant reductions on lamps".

This is equally true of non-sale events. You're inviting me to your housewares show? Don't tell me that I'll see every new convenience. Tell me I'll see new pots that don't have to be watched, new ovens that use less gas.

We need to know whether you're looking for a phone response, a mail response, a mail-and-phone response to your commercial, or if you want the listeners to come running in.

The writing technique is quite different in each case.

We ought to warn you at this point that if you expect direct action via mail or phone, your item must not only be communicable, but instantly communicable. A record, a digital clock, a fragrance, a bed pillow maybe. As simple as that. Or a reupholstery or carpeting special (where you expect inquiries rather than immediate sales).

Nothing the customer prefers to see, to touch, to try on. Nothing where color is important. Nothing where a list of sizes is important. Like sheets.

The commercial: the problems

There are the problems we have when writing your commercials. You should know about them and understand them, so you'll realize why we do certain things.

Since listeners can't go back to your radio ad the way a reader can go back to your print ad, we must repeat. And repeat. And repeat

We must name the store several times. Otherwise they won't know where to buy it. There's no logotype.

We must mention the item several times. They may not have been interested the first time.

If we include a phone number, that must be repeated twice.

Once you understand this, you can see why we can't handle 3 or 4 items in a half minute. We're actually doing each one several times over.

There's also a need for quick identification. To make people turn on their ears and listen. To know that this is news from your store, even before you get into your message. That's why so many commercials start with theme music or sound effects or a phrase used every time around, or a special voice.

The whole identification problem is more difficult on radio where there's no art work, no type style, no layout, no logotype that gives your ad its personality.

The use of some kind of theme, some kind of identification strengthens your commercial because it makes it recognizable as yours.

Commercials are written to a very strict word count. In print, if there are too many words, you can make the size of the type smaller to accomodate them. But you can't stretch a minute or half minute.

If we give the announcer too many words for the time, he'll race through them. You've heard that kind of radio spot . . . the announcer pounding away like a punch press so he can beat the clock. Hardly the climate that makes a customer want to shop. And the message gets lost in the rush.

A 10-second spot (called an ID . . . identification) has no more than 30 short words. Preferably 25.

A half-minute spot will allow you 75 words at the outside.

A one minute spot 150 words.

We needn't point out that this depends on the words. You can get more one syllable words into a commercial than polysyllabic ones.

Therefore, when you're given a commercial to approve, never, never add words, unless you subtract words at the same time. Better yet, count the syllables. You can substitute "mult-i-tude" for "a few of", for example. The smart way to handle it is to sit down with the writer and work it out together. Explain what you want and let the writer worry about the words and the word count.

Since a commercial is meant to be heard rather than read, the best way to judge it is to read it aloud. Then ask yourself:

Is the language easy? Is the sentence construction simple? Does it paint a word picture? Does it sound the way people talk? Is the store mentioned frequently enough for identification? Does it include an urge to take action?

Footnote: One of the characteristics of radio is that humor can be used effectively. Maybe because it's so fast . . . in one ear and out the other. A joke wears stale when it sits in front of you on the printed page. Most writers know this and often use humor in radio commercials. Just make sure that there's not so much humor that your message gets lost.

The 1 minute vs. the 30 seconds

It is extremely difficult to keep your audience listening for a full minute when you use only one voice. They get bored and turn off their ears. It can be done, but it takes tremendous skill.

If your commercial is live rather than taped (see below), you can only use one voice. This, in itself, would be a reason for using 30 seconds rather than the minute.

You're usually better off taking twice as many 30-second spots, since this will give you twice as much exposure.

You're always better off doing two 30-second spots when you have two items. Do each one well, rather than putting them together. By the time you've finished the second item, they'll have forgotten the first.

When, then, is the one minute spot preferable? When you have a commercial that's irresistible listening. Hard to judge, of course. But you can test it for a couple of days and see.

When you can use more than one voice and develop a dialogue or plot. This can be good listening.

When you have real news, and your commercial is a news story. What's happening in your store for Christmas, Building audience for a gigantic sale. A new item that will be demonstrated. Opening of a branch store. Or a remodeled floor. A department or division that you want to push.

You'll notice that these are all semi-institutional in nature. Even though what you're promoting may be at sale prices. You should include a specific item at a specific price in each. How else can you check the effectiveness of your message?

When all other factors indicate a 30-second spot, but you have too much to say for 75 words, don't switch to a minute. Simplify your message instead.

Trick: Very often 1-minute spots are a better buy than 30 seconds. So much better that they're irresistible. That does not, however, mean that you must do 1-minute commercials. You can do two 30's. One after the next. What we call back-to-back. Two individual spots, handled as though each were running on its own. Like a stack of 2 ads.

This not only lets you run more merchandise in your 1-minute spot, but has other advantages as well.

You can rotate the halves. So one day you'll have dresses and shoes, the next dresses and skirts. Or, being totally unrelated spots, you can even have a chair and a blazer.

It eliminates the danger of a potentially dull and long-winded minute. On a subject that only rates 30 seconds.

It lets you talk merchandise in one half and an institutional message in the other. The stories you rarely get to tell on radio. A good way to use part of that thrifty minute.

The 10-second ID

It's a rare item, indeed, that can be promoted in 25 or so words (including store identification). It can be done, but it's a bit of a trick. Mostly in selecting the proper merchandise. It must be identifiable without description . . . no sizes, no colors, not even facts.

For example: tennis balls or golf balls. Or a group of merchandise where the variety is implicit. For example: men's ties at a single price.

The ideal use of the ID is for a store event. Anything from a pre-in-ventory furniture clearance to the personal appearance of a celebrity. As a quick reminder to listeners.

Live vs. tape

This choice is probably not yours. However, you ought to know the advantages and disadvantages of each.

Tape is less flexible. You can't prepare it or change it as fast as you can a live commercial.

On the other hand, you can use any number of voices on tape, which makes for a more interesting commercial. You can always use the same voice or voices, which gives you identification. You can have music and sound effects. You can fuss with tape, do takes and retakes until it's perfect. But unless you plan to use the same spot over and over, it may be uneconomical.

The live commercial, read by the station announcer, is, as we have said, the most flexible of media. You can have one commercial in the morning and a different one on the same subject in the after-noon . . . at no extra cost. You can prepare it in a hurry, if necessary.

The live commercial has an immediacy, an urgency, a news quality built into it because it's done by the familiar station voice.

However, you're limited to one voice. You must take the voice the station gives you. Whichever announcer is on duty at that time.

These days, you may be able to ask for a woman announcer, but what if no woman is working at the hours your spot is aired?

A nice combination is a live voice, plus a bit of taped music or sound effect at the beginning to give you quick identification. This is pos-sible on most, but not all, radio stations. Your station should be asked about it.

Jingles, music, etc.

Unless you are a heavy, consistent advertiser on radio, jingles are probably not for you. Sure, they give identification. But unless your audience has heard your jingle hundreds of times, chances are they will not understand every word. Your name and a little phrase to music (Jones & Jones . . . we have it all) could be fine. But don't try to sell in a jingle. It's a waste of precious air time.

Everybody wants a theme song. It's not an unmixed blessing, however. Consider this. If you're on an all-music station, when your theme comes on, the listeners may think it's just another song. And not turn on their ears! Sound effects might be more provocative and productive. Music on a talk station, by all means. On a music station, to be handled with care.

CHAPTER 16
BROADCAST: TV

Television is such a specialized business that many stores use outside agencies, rather than their own advertising departments, to produce their commercials, and to place them. The agency is also in a better position to buy time slots. They buy more than any one store, since they buy for all their clients. So they have more clout.

Other than the tremendous technical demands of the medium, these stores want to take no chances. A TV commercial is expensive. To produce. To air. So it must be right.

An ad has a one-time life. A TV commercial is used over and over again. So it must be right.

That's why so many stores turn to the experts.

But, whether your store does its TV spots inside or outside, you will be selecting the merchandise. You will be approving the commercial. You should, therefore, know what goes into a good TV ad.

Let's start, as we did with radio, by telling you what a retail TV commercial is not.

It's not an illustrated radio commercial. The problems and the techniques are completely different.

It's not show biz. You don't have to produce a 30-second soap opera to hold your audience. What you put on the tube is news to your customers . . . and can be presented as news. Without a plot. Without all the trappings of theatre. The thing that should be dramatized is the merchandise.

Then what *is* a good TV commercial? *Like any other retail ad, it sells. An item, an idea, an image.* It gives the customer benefits, the reasons why to buy, the specific facts, and urges them into your store. And takes advantage of the medium, the fact that TV has color and motion, and comes across live and real.

Its combination of words, pictures, and action make TV a unique selling tool . . . for some things. It also creates some unique problems.

Warning: Don't confuse retail and national TV. In other words, don't judge your commercial by Alka Seltzer or Campbell soup. You're not selling a product name or product line. To be bought when viewers get into any store. You're trying to bring customers into your store. Now. A whole different bag of tricks.

Warning: Don't think one commercial a day, even in prime time, will do you much good. Repeat! Saturate! Vertical saturation (many spots in one or two days) is better for retail stores than horizontal (a spot or two for many days).

The merchandise

TV is motion. You need merchandise that's not only graphic but also lends itself to movement. We don't just show a coat. We show it being twirled, swirled, being put on or taken off, being cuddled in. (Here's where you can ask us to show both the back and front . . . and we'll never say no!). Fashion in action.

What if you have a can of paint, a set of dishes? We'll add people, if we can afford them. Yes, we can show a close-up of the can, but you're not using TV properly unless we also show someone painting. Yes, we can show the pattern of the dishes, but it's better if we show someone setting the table.

You can have a washing machine and a pitchman describing its wonders (you've seen *that* commercial), but you'll catch more eyes if someone is using the washer. Remember . . . it's what it does rather than the machine itself that's important to the viewer.

TV shows it like it is. Merchandise is not interpreted by the artist. It's not retouched as a photograph can be.

That means every accessory must be just right.

That means, if it's fashion, you must provide the proper size for the model and it must be fitted exactly. You can't fake on TV.

If it's a home scene, you must provide everything from the rug to the picture on the wall.

90

You shouldn't depend on the TV studio for even a pair of shoes or a napkin ring. You're making a total statement so you should control everything that's shown, even if it's visible for only a split second.

Since most TV commercials are now in color, this must also be considered when you select merchandise. Not just the item itself, but how it's accessorized. The camera often does funny things to colors, so ask the TV experts. Or give them a choice.

How much merchandise?

Because TV is so expensive, you may feel that you have to expose more goods to justify it. Don't.

Because it shows the merchandise and doesn't require the descriptions you need on radio, you may think you can cram it with a lot of stuff. You're wrong.

A commercial is not a picture book with pages to be flipped in a hurry. At least, not if you're using it properly.

You not only want to show merchandise, but you want to sell it. You want the viewer to remember it, to come in and buy it.

A quick glimpse is not enough to whet the buying appetite, not enough time for the words that are necessary to bring customers into your store, eager to buy. And if you expect mail or phone response, that limits the number of items you can show even more drastically. Ideally to one.

How many pieces of goods can go into a 30-second commercial? There's no easy answer to this. It depends. On whether you expect to sell specific merchandise or an idea.

If there's a common denominator, you can show several things. If they're basically the same style . . . like folding chairs or men's slacks or kid's jeans. If the story's the same . . . like easy-care quilted bedspreads. Or the same price . . . like a choice of mink coats at $2000 . . . or tables at $99. If they have any of these, you may be able to show and sell 3 effectively in a half minute. Maybe even 4 . . . if the price is the same. It depends. On how much you have to show to communicate. On how much you have to say to sell.

When you're selling an idea, whether it's a new fashion idea, an assortment, or something like a big sale, you can expose a lot of goods. But don't expect to sell any individual item. Or a lot of prices. Just the idea of come and see them all.

When you're selling an item that must be demonstrated, or has a lot of facts . . . a sofa bed, for example, or a service like custom slipcovers, your 30 seconds is barely enough time for one thing.

Facts

TV is a 3-ring circus. You have the picture (the video), the voice or voices (audio) and the words shown on the screen (the super, short for superimposed). You cannot have all three going at once without bewildering the viewer. There must be a breather, when they can look at the merchandise without having words hurled at them.

That means fewer words. Which, in turn, means that you must edit your facts carefully to include only the major consumer benefits.

By all means provide the writer with every fact. This supplies background, story, and starts our imagination working. But indicate the most important ones clearly. And limit those to just a few.

If your drapery story is primarily drip-dry, don't ask us to describe every pattern in detail.

If your story is fur-trimmed coats, don't ask us to spell out every fabric and fabric blend.

Concentrate on the essentials, the basic selling points. And skip anything that can be seen in the picture. What's the reason for saying long-sleeved if the long sleeves show? (Unless that's the fashion news.)

We surely don't have to remind you that there should be no also-rans. If they don't see it on the tube, they won't come in and buy it. Or wide price ranges. Unless you're also pricing the actual items shown.

Identification

A 30-second commercial does not give you 30 seconds for your merchandise. Part of your time must be spent telling viewers where to buy it. In audio and video. Words and some form of logotype or name and address.

Like radio, there is no turning back to see where the merchandise can be bought.

And like any other form of advertising, there must be the more subtle form of identification as well. The commercial must reflect your store. Merchandise, personality, point of view.

Lead time

A TV commercial takes a long time to prepare. Usually from 4 to 6 weeks. Or even longer.

It is very much a team job, never the creation of one person.

It is a complex job, from storyboard or script to casting to rehearsals to taping or filming to developing, cutting, editing. Hollywood on a small scale.

Sometimes, if it doesn't go right and the client is very critical (which the client . . . the store . . . should be), a studio can spend a full day just taking and re-taking a few seconds.

If the commercial is filmed on location instead of in a studio, there's a lot of gear to transport, a lot of scouting locations and often you must get permission to film. Then you may have to sit out bad weather. And pay your models . . . and the rest of the crew . . . portal to portal.

All this is part of the reason why a TV commercial costs. It takes a surprisingly large number of people. It takes a lot of time.

It can, of course, be done in a hurry . . . sometimes. Years ago, when Macy's did line-for-line copies of import fashions, we used to tape a whole half-hour show in a day. Admittedly, a long day. With solid weeks of work behind it, selecting the fashions, writing the script, casting the models, developing a format with the director, fitting, accessorizing.

Why the rush? We wanted to be on TV as soon as we could after the fashions arrived from Europe.

So it can be done, but it's not a good idea.

Changes

Once your commercial is in the can, it's almost impossible to change it. Make your changes on the storyboard, on the script, even while it's being filmed or edited. Because once it's done, it's done. Especially if it's on tape. You can patch film a little, change a slide or a super . . . but it costs plenty. On tape . . . it's harder to do at any price.

If your store does a lot of TV, take the time to watch a commercial being made. Enlightening.

How to judge a TV commercial

It's not easy. The medium is so dazzling, with such show-biz overtones that we all tend to fall for the sheer glamour of it. And feel like an impressario.

Also, it takes an experienced eye to judge the potential of a commercial from a script or a storyboard. The action is missing. The unique quality of the medium.

Like any other form of advertising, however, there are basic questions you can ask yourself.

Does it give the merchandise news . . . look like news, sound like news?

Does it spell out the customer benefits . . . is there a reason to come buy?

Will the merchandise look good?

Will the merchandise be seen . . . or is it so overwhelmed by plot or action that it will be hard to tell what you're selling?

Does it have an urge to action . . . or does it merely state the case?

Does it give enough specific facts to turn the viewer into a customer . . . or is it merely mood music?

Does it give the viewer time to absorb what you're showing and saying . . . or is it so jam-packed that it will race past?

Is it completely clear that this is *your* store's TV ad?

And . . . the question to ask of all advertising . . . would it sell me?

The canned commercial

Because the TV commercial started from scratch is so expensive, your store may buy commercials from companies that produce them and sell the same commercials to many stores. This amortizes the cost. It means you can buy professionally produced . . . and the production is almost invariably excellent . . . commercials for far less than you can produce them.

These companies go to markets, work with national manufacturers, use top-flight talent, and frequently film in exotic locations.

All your store has to do is "supers" with your logotype, your prices, or a special message.

That's what your store *has* to do. But it's not what your store *ought* to do. Not if you want the commercial to work hard for you.

You can't touch the video but, as we said, the video is almost always superb. Your advertising people, however, should prepare a new script and tape it. Since "voice-over" (a voice talking while the picture is being shown) is usually used, this is a relatively small deal.

Why a new script? These commercials are used by many stores so, of necessity, are general. The way to make them your own is with your words. Talking to your customer in your language, as you do in other advertising. By selling your store as well as the goods. By adding urgency.

If your store is not doing this to canned commercials, talk to your advertising manager. It's simple to do, and it pays off.

When a canned commercial is used, you still OK the merchandise in it. Ask yourself . . . is this the merchandise I would choose if I were planning a TV commercial? Is it typical of my merchandise? Do I have enough stock to support the commercial . . . or do I have to go out and buy some? Is it at *all* our stores? If the answers are "no", do some communing with yourself and the ad department.

"Available At"

One of your vendors has bought a "flight" of spots on your local TV station. Since he wants action as well as exposure, he'll offer to identify your store as the place to buy his goods. The last frame of the commercial will say "Available at Blah-Blah" or something like that.

Does this do you any good?

Well, it's free. And you may get some business out of it if it's a wanted item. You'll also keep your name in front of the TV-viewing public.

But, like any other piece of vendor advertising where you have no control over the content . . . be careful.

Ask that you and your ad department see the commercial in advance. Or, if it's not prepared yet, the storyboard and script.

To make sure it doesn't say anything you wouldn't say in your own advertising. That it's in tune with store policy. That it doesn't take potshots at other goods you carry. That it's right for your store, your market.

If it's OK (and most of them are . . . we don't want to scare you), then you've got yourself a nice gift.

More arithmetic

We told you about the extra pull of a combination of radio and print. Use a combo of all 3 media . . . print, radio, and TV . . . and the arithmetic is even more interesting. 1+1+1=5. Worth thinking about, especially when you're opening a new store or floor, launching a new product, or starting a major store-wide event.

CHAPTER 17

HOW TO MEASURE ADVERTISING RESULTS

As advertising people, we like to know how customers respond to the ads we produce. It's one of the reasons we're in retail advertising. Instead of some lush plush ad agency. The satisfaction of knowing that our ads make people react. Immediately.

We could find out the response by going to the selling floor and counting bodies. Many of us do.

But one quick look-see at 11 a.m. doesn't really tell the story. So we call you on the phone.

When you answer, please don't give us generalities or expletives.

Like "I don't know". What a let down!

Or "Pretty good". Which is frustrating. It tells us nothing.

"Lousy". Well, how bad is lousy? Didn't anything sell?

"Great" is equally non-specific. Business is obviously jumping, but how good is great? A half dozen customers or a mob scene?

And, of course, there's always "Sold out". At 11 a.m.?

Instead, tell us "It opened strong . . or weak . . or too early to tell. Call you back at 4 p.m." And don't forget to call us back (Of course, if you can give us figures that early in the day, we'd love them.)

The real answer, however, comes the day after the ad has run. Or 2 days, 3 days, or even a week. Depending on the type of promotion and the amount of promotional support.

Surely, we needn't add that it's not only important for the advertising department to know how well the ad produced (or didn't), but it's important for you, too. In the most minute detail.

What we should both know about measuring ad results

There are many advertising ideas and many ways to present these ideas. They have one common denominator. Every ad should bring a measurable response. If it doesn't, your work and ideas are wasted. Ditto ours.

However, you should understand what kind of response to expect. Depending on whether the ad puts its emphasis on volume, on profit, or on prestige. Each category is subject to different modes of measurement of response.

Measuring the results of institutional ads

As you know, this is advertising that creates and maintains the store's reputation and personality. It relates the store to the community, to contemporary events, to its services and personnel, to its merchandise superiorities and even to its pricing policies.

Institutional advertising simply can't be measured on the next day's or next week's sale sheet. Nor should it be. It can only be measured in decades. Really. By the respect of customers, suppliers, and stockholders. By the way a store grows. And thrives. And profits.

Measuring the results of indirect advertising

This is the bulk of advertising for most non-promotional stores.

Very simply, it's advertising that creates and maintains the store's reputation . . . through its merchandise. The new, the now, the exclusive. All at regular prices or at full mark-on. Advertising that exposes superior assortments, superior quality, or superior design.

Indirect advertising can bring an immediate response. However, final results should be tallied over a period of a week, a month, or a season. Not the next day. After all, you're not asking them to zoom in.

With this big exception. There's a visible relationship between how much your customers want the goods and the speed with which they respond. Warm gloves during a cold wave or smoke detectors after a rash of local fires, advertised at regular prices, will bring them in. Pronto. A new skirt length or a new fashion idea (ready-to-wear or home furnishings) will be slower.

Indirect advertising also provides an important peripheral benefit, a gauge of consumer demand. An indication, straight from the customers, of what they like, want, and will buy. This can be translated into both strong stock positions and advertising emphasis. And should be.

Measuring the results of direct advertising

Clearances, storewide and department sales, item sales, special purchases. Off-price. That's direct advertising. Reflecting the price and value policy of the store. Either planned or purely opportunistic.

Direct advertising should bring an immediate response. The next day or during the period of the event. The shorter this period, the better. For example, a 3-day sale is more urgent, hence has more propulsion power, than a 2-week sale.

Another form of direct advertising: merchandise with smaller than normal mark-ons even if the tell-tale words like "Sale" and "Special Purchase" are not used.

Many stores, as a matter of policy, will not allow the words "Sale" to be used unless the merchandise is marked down by at least 10%. These are usually hot communicable items whose value at the new lower prices is obvious.

The mass merchandisers' advertising is also direct. Whether they use comparatives or not, whether they say "sale" or not, the total appeal is a value appeal. More for less money.

Like the more traditional sales, all this advertising should bring an immediate response. And should be measured in a period of one day or, at most, one week.

Note: A recent survey by the Newspaper Advertising Bureau reveals that 60% of all newspaper ads are promotional. Direct advertising in one form or another. This includes, of course, all ads. From supermarkets to specialty shops.

Formulas for measuring advertising results

Over the years, some more-or-less standard formulas have evolved. Sure, they're useful. They can be used as guides. But each store should establish its own performance formula. Based on its own experience, its own market situation.

There are just too many variables, store to store, market to market, to set up rigid rules. What kind of variables? Well, here are some. All of which affect advertising results. Your store may have other special situations.

1. The amount and kind of advertising a store runs.
2. Customer acceptance of the store.
3. The competition and competition's advertising.
4. What media are available; how good (or bad) media coverage is.
5. Store location: lots or little traffic.
6. The time of the year re the advertised merchandise.
7. Local business conditions. National and international, too.
8. The weather
9. Front page news.
10. Store services like credit, phone, parking, etc.
11. The desirability of the merchandise advertised.

Traditional department stores use a formula of 10 to 1 for their direct (off-price) advertising. For every dollar invested, they look for a minimum return of ten dollars. An ad that costs $500, for example, should bring in $5000 in volume during the life of the promotion.

Aggressively promotional stores, with constant sales and events, usually expect a 6 to 1 response to direct advertising.

Specialy shops and non-promotional non-department stores consider a 3 or 4 or 5 to 1 ratio a good response to direct advertising depending on the number and frequency of events. The more sales, the smaller the results. Although a major event like a season or year end clearance can push the ratio up to 10 or 15 to 1 or even higher.

Indirect advertising has never had a specific formula. The ratio of cost to volume depends too much on the nature of the merchandise. An item that's a proven runner is one thing, but as we've said, a new idea is another. Slower. Even though the new idea may be essential to polishing the store's image. Results, therefore, can vary from 2 to 1 to 5 to 1.

As a result, many stores use the P.O.N. measurement: the plus-over-normal business for the item advertised or even for the department. The time of measurement is usually a week.

What advertising results can tell you

Believe it or not, they can tell you more about your business trends than your monthly computer read-out. It's not after the fact. It's *the* fact!

That's why it's so important to keep accurate and complete records of your advertising. It's so simple. It takes so little time.

Just keep a file book of your ads. Then alongside each ad, write the following:
- Date the ad ran, the medium, the size, the cost.
- Volume produced by the ad. Day by day for the length of the promotion.
- The department's volume, versus same time last year.
- Number of units sold. Which sold best . . . by size, style, and color.
- The percentage of cost of the ad vis-a-vis volume.
- Note the weather, competitors' advertising and unusual factors. Like front page news.

These facts are essential to you . . and the store. In planning merchandise replacements and future promotions.

What advertising results can tell the ad department

We can learn from our successes . . and our failures. The advertising department should have the same facts on each ad that you have. Because these facts can answer many questions quickly.

- Was the merchandise decision right or wrong?
- Was the price right?
- Were the ad techniques good?
- Did the copy tell the story?
- Did the art show the merchandise to its best advantage?
- Would we do the ad the same way? If we had another chance?
- Would we use the same media?
- Would we use the same timing?

If the ad was a tremendous success, we should be on the phone asking you "Can we get more of the same merchandise? How soon? Can we repeat the ad? When can we repeat it?"

That's when having the facts pays off. In a hurry!

CHAPTER 18

HOW TO JUDGE COPY WITHOUT BEING A WRITER

How can you tell whether copy is good, very good, or bad? Here are some questions to ask yourself.

Does the headline give the news . . . or is it merely a label? Think of the difference between "White is here for winter" and "White Winter Coats". The picture will show coats, won't it?

Does the ad give the customer benefits . . . or is it self-serving? Think of the difference between "Reduced 30%" (what you're doing) and "You save 30%" (what the customer is getting).

Does the ad talk YOU . . . rather than US?

Does the ad give a reason for buying, or does it merely catalogue the facts? Bullet copy has its place, but it's not the ideal way to sell. You can't create an emotional climate with bullet copy.

Does the ad give a reason for buying at *your* store? Don't send them to your competition!

Is your ad topical and timely . . . or so bland that it slides past the reader? If the same ad could have been written in the same language last year . . . where have you been?

Is the language fresh, upbeat, and interesting . . . or is it cliche-filled and plain dull?

Does the ad include all the necessary facts to make a buying decision . . . or are you making it hard for the customer to shop? Before you decide this one, read the ad as though you'd never seen the merchandise before.

Does the ad involve the customers . . . talk to them in their own frame of reference, to their interests. Do you know to whom you're talking?

103

Is the ad as specific as it can be made . . . or is it so general that it really says nothing?

Is the ad honest . . . or is it full of poetic license? Can you back every claim?

Is the ad recognizable as *your* ad . . . the language, the approach, the style . . . or could it be anybody's ad?

Would it sell *you?*

CHAPTER 19

HOW TO JUDGE GRAPHICS WITHOUT BEING
A DESIGNER OR ARTIST

This is somewhat harder than judging copy, because we all like a pretty picture. But here are some questions to ask when you look at an ad.

Does the ad have a focal point . . . or is everything so evenly spaced that there's nothing to grab your eye?

Does the art look like your store and reflect your store's personality . . . or is it out of character with everything you stand for?

Is the art in proper relationship to the copy . . . or are you giving too much space to a long copy story when the art will do the selling . . . or wasting space on a big meaningless picture when words can do a better selling job?

Does the eye follow from element to element naturally . . . or are there a lot of irrelevant elements and gimmicks that stop the reader from reading?

Are you trying to tell too many stories in the ad . . . or do you have a simple easy-to-grasp message?

Are your art and copy in the same sequence . . . or are you asking the reader to hunt and pick?

Is your use of color meaningful to the merchandise . . . or are you using color merely for the sake of color?

Is your store's signature cut legible, easy to find, and consistent with store policy . . . or does your ad look anonymous?

Is everything so big that the reader can't see anything?

Have you merchandised your ad so it results in a clean-cut direct story . . . or have you given the ad department a hodge-podge to work with?

Is all merchandise priced . . . or are you making it hard for customers to know what they get for their money?

Is the art doing something for you . . . or would you be better off with a dramatic all-type ad?

Can you read the ad . . . even if you don't have 20-20 vision?

Would the ad bring *you* into the store?

CHAPTER 20

WORKING WITH AGENCIES, MEDIA STAFFS, CONSULTANTS

In other words, how to work with people who don't work for your store. But with you. To create ads.

You'll get a lot better product if you disregard this distinction and consider them part of the extended family. That means: don't hold out. Confide in them. Tell them your problems, your aspirations. Even the skeletons in the closet. The more we know (and here we both talk as long-time consultants for many stores), the better the job we can do for you. This is true even if you only want a series of jazzy little institutionals. Which don't come out of creative heads, but start with hard facts.

At the same time, don't let yourself be bullied. Or dazzled by creative pyrotechnics. After all, you know your merchandise, your customer, your market, your competition. But don't resist new ideas either, or new approaches. Merely because you've never done them before. The person you're working with, whether it's a radio station copywriter or a consultant, is an advertising pro. With a contribution to make.

We believe that the best investment for a store doing a reasonable amount of advertising is an advertising department of its own. (A reasonable amount is a couple of ads a week, a batch of radio spots, and a few pieces of direct mail a year. For any store earning a satisfactory profit on sales of a million or more.) Such an ad department can be only one person. Writer, designer, manager, coordinator, it doesn't matter. As long as there's a body on the premises whose main job is to watch over the advertising. Whose loyalty is, first and foremost, to the store.

Unless there is such a person, chances are the store owner is acting like an ad manager. Taking on a job for which he has few professional qualifications. Running to and from the agency or newspaper or broadcast station. We even know a few stores where the boss actually pastes down artwork or writes copy. The ads look it, too! On a cost efficiency basis, he could probably spend his time more profitably and afford to hire an advertising person. Except that a) it hasn't occurred to him that he's big enough for such a move and b) he's having so much fun.

With no ad department, the ads are usually done by an agency or the media. Whom you have to work with directly. Even if there is an ad department, the store may often choose to have broadcast (especially TV) done by a studio or station.

Note: In everything we say below, we'd like to point out that we are deliberately taking the most cynical point of view. There are many agencies and media staffs that turn out retail ads that are superior to what any person you'd hire could do. And watch your budget as if it were their own. Unfortunately, there's the other kind, too. So we think you should be warned.

Agencies

Working with them:
Unless it's a tiny agency where the principals double as writers and designers, you'll work with an account executive. A surrogate ad manager. When you get down to actual ads, ask to have the writer present at meetings. So your information won't have to be channeled through a third party.

Treat the agency as though it were your own ad department. Needless to say, if it's a new agency for the store, it should get to know the store. Thoroughly. Beyond that, brief the agency on the background of every ad: what you expect it to accomplish, who it's aimed at, how it fits into the store's position and merchandise philosophy.

Provide all the facts for every ad. Let the agency see the merchandise, if possible. Don't wait for the last minute; stay on schedule. They do have other accounts to service, you know.

Make yourself available for questions and to look at ads. Don't wait till an ad is on proof or tape to review it. Ask for copy and layouts . . . in advance.

If you're unhappy with an ad, don't make it a personal matter, but a business problem. If you're delighted with the ad, tell them so. Even more loudly.

Note to bosses: Sit down with your agency before each season and make a firm plan. Work with them to decide on which media, how much space, and when ads should run. Don't ask them to come up with a campaign . . . out of the air. Or you'll get something that's precisely that: all air. Be sure they know your objectives, the number of dollars you plan to spend, and what return you expect for those dollars.

What to watch out for:
The major hazard in using an agency is that some of them don't know the retail business. Or understand the basics of retail advertising. Their ads tend to be impersonal and general. The objective is to attract attention (good) rather than sell merchandise (bad). Nor do they understand the need to sell the store as a place to shop.

If your agency is not retail-oriented, you may end up with eye-catching or ear-catching national-type ads. That do you very little good. To avoid this, you'll simply have to teach them about retailing and retail advertising. If you're not sure about the distinction between national and retail advertsing yourself, you have a real problem on your hands.

As a small client, you may find you're getting the newest staff members doing your ads. This may not be as bad as it sounds; depending on their talents and your guidance, they may turn out great ads. Or you may get minimal attention from the agency. A more serious situation. Be a squeaky wheel. Be a bit of a pest. Your ads are just as important to you as the big spenders' are to them. Don't overdo it, of course.

Don't let yourself be overawed by fancy presentations (or fancy offices). It's content that counts. Examine your ads critically. To make sure they work for *you*. That they reflect your store. They're pitched to your customer.

Note to bosses: Often spending more money on advertising will bring in greater profits. Sometimes it only fattens the agency. Proceed with caution.

If your agency is more comfortable in one medium than others, say radio vs. newspaper, your media picture could be distorted. Again, proceed with caution.

Anything said above, naturally, can be avoided by choosing the right agency.

The media staff

Working with them:
We've discovered that media creative staffs are the most over-worked and under-appreciated of people. They rarely have time to research, reflect, or dig out material. They lean heavily on what you provide. So provide material generously. Over-generously. Preferably to the person doing your ads, rather than a media rep. Who, like the account execitive, is a go-between.

Don't wait for the rep to come see you with an "idea". Gather your facts and go down to th paper or broadcast office. Explain, discuss, confer with the creative people, then follow up.

When you work with a newspaper, ask them to develop a series of formats for your ads. So you can merchandise to them. It will be easier for all.

When you work with broadcast stations, be there when they tape. (See Chapters 15 and 16.) Ask for copies of commercials for your ad book. Monitor the spots personally from time to time.

Otherwise, everything we said about working with agencies applies. Except that, happily, most media understand retail.

Watch out for:
Each medium is a self-centered unit. It has to be. So if you're using more than one medium, be sure you don't have a different face, a different personality in each. It will be up to you to coordinate the effort and, especially, to make sure that campaigns are seamless.

If media creative staff is doing a half-dozen stores in town, a certain sameness may creep in. It's only natural. Every writer and designer has a style: pet phrases and arrangements. When you see this happen, cry stop! Ask them to reconsider your ads totally in the context of your store's personality.

Note to bosses: Each medium will try to prove to you that it reaches more people and gives you more for your money. So you'd better increase their budget, at the expense of other media. They may be right. They may be wrong. This is a decision you should make on your own. After listening, scrutinizing, and evaluating the facts.

Consultants

Working with them:
They come in 2 varieties: the outsider brought in to examine your advertising or the outsider who comes in and actually helps create, or at least spark, the ads. In either case, it's usually an expert. Someone who will take a cold impersonal experienced look at your advertising. And whose conclusions will probably shake you up.

Brief your consultant exhaustively. Including even facts you consider self-evident. For example, you may take shopping patterns in your town for granted. That's all you know. But they may be unique to your town. So leave no stone unturned. Give the consultant the broadest base on which to make recommendations and judgements.

A consultant on a continuing basis is usually more productive than a series of different consultants. Why? First of all, it takes time for a consultant to know the store. Then, while you may get some great ideas from one visit, the big thing a consultant can do is keep your ads from sliding back into the familiar rut. It's been our experience that the ideas and inspiration of a consultant have a life-span of about 2 to 3 months.

To get the most out of your consultant, he or she should see every advertising and sales promotion plan and property. Well in advance. If this isn't feasible, then they can be critiqued after the fact. And the comments in said critiques noted for future use.

Watch out for:
Your advertising consultant may get so involved, you'll get advice on matters that have little to do with ads. Like how to arrange your stock. This may be good. Or bad. Just be wary.

Your consultant may come complete with a set of ideas and notions that have been proven at other stores. Fundamentally sound, but not applicable to all stores. Again, be wary. While advertising principles are the same, some interpretations don't travel well. What works in one market area may be a dud in another.

111

If you bring in a consultant and have either an ad staff or an agency, you may create resentment. This can be avoided, but it takes tactful footwork. By you and the consultant.

A last word on consultants. The store is paying for their advice. If you agree with the advice, it should be heeded. Totally. Taking one part of a plan because you like it and ignoring the rest, may invalidate the whole thing. Then be patient. Allow time for new ideas, new directions to work. It may be a couple of months before you see measurable results.

CHAPTER 21

HOW THE BEST ADS ARE CREATED

You may not realize it, but you've just had a short course in advertising. Not enough to turn you into a copywriter or a designer, but enough of the basic principles so you understand what retail advertising is about. How we work. And what we are trying to do. For you.

The better you understand this, the better your ads will be.

Because the best retail ads are not created by one individual, but by a team: writer, designer, and merchant.

Sitting down together to examine the merchandise problem and establish a point of view.

Sitting down together to explore the possibilities, the approaches, the angles.

You will say this takes time. It does. But it's time well spent if it makes your ads produce more business. You don't have to have a conference on every ad, but certainly on all major ads and on campaigns. And when we say conference, we mean it in the literal sense of the word. A bringing together. Of minds. Of ideas.

The results will more than pay for your investment in time. And ours.

There are several other things you can and should do.

Encourage your advertising department to experiment, to try new ways of handling the same old things.

Be ruthless about ads that do nothing for your store. It's better to have fewer ads but good ads. One dramatic ad with real impact and real sell can be more effective than 3 so-what ads.

Get your advertising people involved in what's happening in your department, your store. Make them part of *your* team. Tell them your long-range plans. Tell them when there are new merchandise developments, new trends. Tell them how an ad does. Give them the facts and the figures, yours and your competition's.

If we, as advertising people, have failed to communicate, you have failed too. So often, the only time you call us is when you have a complaint. Why don't you call us to praise our good ads? To tell us what's going on?

Most important of all, because merchandising and advertising are interdependent, make them interdisciplinary.

Talk to the brass; talk to the training department. See if you can't find a way to teach merchants about advertising and your advertising people about merchandising.

Set up sessions, formal or informal, so you can learn about one another's problems and be able to work together more efficiently as a team. Do it not once, but on a continuing basis.

Then your ads will sing!

A last word

The best ad in the world can't sell merchandise that people don't want, is of poor quality, or overpriced. All that a good ad can really do is move more of the merchandise that they want. Merchandise that's timely, well-priced, and properly made.

This is not an alibi. It's a fact, proven many times over. Which is why we call the merchant the secret ingredient of good ads.

CHAPTER 22

GLOSSARY OF ADVERTISING LANGUAGE

Like any business, advertising has a special technical language. To help you talk to (and understand) the advertising department, we're listing the more commonly used terms. Some are in the text, but we've also included them here for quick reference. They're divided into print (newspapers, magazines, mailings, etc.), radio, and TV because each speaks its own tongue.

AGATE LINE: Measurement used by newspapers, one column wide and one-fourteenth of an inch deep.

BENDAY OR BEN DAY: A mechanical engraving process that superimposes gray tones on a line drawing. It comes in many tones and textures.

CAMERA LUCIDA: An instrument (familiarly known as a Lucy) used by artists and designers. For drawing subjects from life, copying art, enlarging, or reducing, or reversing.

CENTER: All lines of type are centered, leaving various widths to the left and right. Used mostly for display type.

CHARACTER COUNT: The number of type characters that will fit into an area in a designated style and size of type. For example 20 x 6 means 20 characters to a line, 6 lines deep.

COLD TYPE: Phototypography. Mostly set by computer on punched tape. The type is then reproduced photographically on film or paper.

COLUMN INCH: Measurement of newspaper space; one column wide, one inch deep.

COMP (COMPREHENSIVE): A hand-made facsimile of an ad, showing the way it will appear in the newspaper.

COPY COUNT: The number of type characters that will fit into an area of the layout, based on the relationship of the size of typewriter type to the type designated.

CROMOLITE: One of several trade-mark products, it's a chemical used by artists instead of water in a "wash drawing". The art is then sprayed with another chemical by the engraver and filtered through the camera lens so reproduction of the half-tone engraving is improved.

DEMOGRAPHICS: Characteristics of an audience (for any medium) by age, sex, occupation, education, economic status, etc.

DISPLAY TYPE: Often called headline or sub-headline type. From 16 pt. up.

DOORBUSTERS: Extraordinary values, usually handled as bold liners in an ad.

DOUBLE TRUCK: Two facing pages treated as a single advertising unit, even when there's a gutter between them (see "gutter").

FIXED LOCATION: The same position in the newspaper, in every issue.

FLUSH LEFT: All lines of type aligned on the left side; random width on the right side.

FLUSH RIGHT: As above, but all lines are aligned on the right side.

GUTTER: The blank space on the inside margins of the newspaper.

HALF-TONE: A reproduction process that translates the gray tones in drawings and photographs into dots.

HOT TYPE: Typography that is set from pre-cast type letter by letter or is machine-set by casting letters, words, or lines from hot metal.

LAYOUT MARK-UP: Information on the layout for the mechanical completion of an ad. This includes such details as type name and size, key letters, the copy, art, logotype, borders, etc.

LEADING: The space between lines of type. "Set Solid" is as tight as the lines can be set.

LINAGE: The number of agate lines of one or more ads in the newspaper.

LINE: One-fourteenth of an inch.

LINE CUT: An engraving that is made from art or type in which the line or the area is solid black.

LINE-FOR-LINE: Copy is set exactly as typed, each line of type ending where the line of typed copy ends.

LOGO: Your store's logotype or signature cut. The name of the store distinctively and consistently used.

MAKE-UP: The arrangement of printed material on a page or in an issue of the newspaper.

MECHANICAL: Camera-ready copy. Every element of the ad is pasted into position, ready for the engraver, in one unit.

MIL LINE RATE: The cost of one line of advertising per million circulation at the lowest line rate, minus space and frequency discounts.

OFFSET PRINTING: A process in which the impression is transferred from an engraving plate to a rubber blanket and then printed on paper.

POINT: There are 72 points to the inch. The point size indicates the height of the type letter.

PREFERRED POSITION: An especially desirable position in the paper. Often at a surcharge; sometimes given to a heavy advertiser.

PRESS RUN: The total number of copies printed.

REVERSE TYPE: White type on black or gray, either background or art.

R-O-P: Run-of-paper position; anywhere in the newspaper. R-O-P color is a color ad placed anywhere in the regular sections of the paper.

SURPRINT TYPE: Black type superimposed over art or a gray area.

VELOX PRINT: Photographic reproduction of original art in a specified size. It can be all line, all half-tone, or a combination.

WAIT ORDER: Sometimes also called Display Order. An ad that is set in type, then held for further instruction.

RADIO

ANNOUNCEMENT: Commercial or spot. Message of 60, 30, or 10 seconds.

AVAILABILITIES: Time slots where commercials can be placed. Often shortened to "avails".

BTA: Best Time Available. Run of schedule. If better times become available, spots are upgraded.

COST PER THOUSAND: The cost for radio time to reach 1000 listeners.

CUMULATIVE AUDIENCE: Also called "cume". Audience reached by a station over an extended period of time.

DRIVE TIME: Usually 6 to 10 a.m. for morning drive time; PM drive time from 4 to 7 p.m. Sometimes called Traffic or Commuter time.

EVENING: Radio time slot that usually runs from 7 p.m. to midnight.

FIXED POSITION: Spot will be delivered at a guaranteed time, say 6:29 p.m. every day. An extra charge for this guarantee.

FLIGHT: A specific and intensive campaign, usually on a single event or idea, within a relatively limited time.

FREQUENCY: Average number of times an advertiser's message reaches an individual in a specific period of time.

HOUSEWIFE TIME: Usually between 10 a.m. and 3 p.m.

ID: Short for identification. A 10-second commercial.

NIGHT TIME: Time slot from midnight to 6 a.m.

OPEN-END: Taped commercial that leaves room at the end for "live" tag.

PREMIUM RATE: Extra charge for special valuable time: fixed position, news, special events, weather, etc.

REACH: The number of different individuals a program or commercial reaches in a given time period or combination of time periods.

REMOTE: A broadcast from some place other than the station's studio.

SATURATION: A heavy schedule of spots to reach as many listeners as possible as quickly as possible.

SHARE OF AUDIENCE: Percentage of tuned-in audience listening to each station at any given time.

TENS: 10-second commercials.

THIRTIES: 30-second commercials.

VERTICAL SATURATION: Slotting commercials heavily on several stations for a limited time to reach maximum number of listeners.

TELEVISION

ACROSS THE BOARD: Spots scheduled at the same time from Monday through Friday or Sunday. A "board" is a week.

ANIMATION: Action imparted to still artwork by shooting it frame by frame.

ANSWER PRINT: First composite film print struck from negative. Equivalent to a proof.

AVERAGE AUDIENCE. Also called AA. Percentage of TV households tuned in to a program during an average minute.

CPM: Cost per thousand. Cost to reach 1000 people or homes.

CLOSE-UP (CU). A very close camera shot, to show detail. Also called a tight shot.

CRAWL: Words or artwork that moves up or down or side to side across the TV screen.

DAY PARTS: Times of telecast. Usually divided into morning, afternoon, early evening, night, and late night.

DISSOLVE: A fade-out of pictures or words while other pictures or words appear. Can be slow or fast.

FIXED RATE: Price for a time slot which guarantees that the commercial will run at that time and not be pre-empted.

FREQUENCY: Average number of times an unduplicated audience viewed a TV schedule.

GROSS RATING POINTS: Also called GRP's. The sum of the audiences for each commercial in a schedule.

HORIZONTAL SATURATION: Intensive schedule of spots at the same time for several days to target an audience that views at that time.

ID: Station identification; also 10-second spot.

KINE: (Pronounced ''Kinny''). Short for kinescope; filming of TV program from a monitor.

LS: Long shot

PIGGY BACK: A long commercial, made up of two short individual commercials for different items, placed back to back.

PRE-EMPTIBLE SPOTS: Commercials sold at reduced rates with the station having the option of selling the time to an advertiser who will pay full rates for that time.

PRIME TIME: Hours between 7:30 p.m. and 11 p.m. in Eastern, Mountain and Pacific time zones; 6:30 to 10 p.m. in Central time zone.

ROS: Run of station. Commercials bought to run at station's discretion at any time of day.

REACH: Number or percent of audience exposed to message.

SATURATION: Heavy use of commercials in a short period of time.

SHARE OF AUDIENCE: The percentage of total TV viewing audience tuned to a program in a given time period.

STORYBOARD: Artwork showing the sequence of a TV commercial, including all major visual scene changes.

SYNC: Matching of sound to picture.

VOICE OVER: When the speaker's voice is broadcast, but the speaker is not shown.

Many of these definitions are based on booklets from the Newspaper Advertising Bureau, Inc., the Radio Advertising Bureau, Inc., and the Television Bureau of Advertising, Inc. All of whom we thank for help in compiling this glossary.

INDEX

accuracy 17, 18, 65, 69
advertising as news 4, 80, 87, 89
advertising department responsibility 2, 3, 23, 24, 25, 26, 27, 29, 73, 95, 113, 114
advertising that sells 1, 4, 104, 105
agencies 108, 109
art instructions 14, 15, 17
all type ads 20, 22, 106
assortment ad 46

bill enclosures 72, 73
booklets 63, 64, 65, 66, 67, 68, 69, 70, 71
broadcast 80, 81, 82, 83, 84, 85, 86, 87, 88, 89, 90, 91, 92, 93, 94, 95, 96
bullet copy 79, 101, 102

"canned" commercials 95
catalogues 63, 64, 65, 66, 67, 68, 69, 70
changes 10, 17, 18, 28, 35, 36, 37, 53, 54, 55, 56, 57, 58, 65, 74, 83, 94
clarity 11
color 33, 64, 90, 105
comparative prices 11, 73
computer letters 74
consultants 111, 112
copy 7, 8, 9, 10, 11, 12, 13, 26, 30, 31, 32, 33, 34, 63, 65, 66, 68, 83, 84, 94, 103, 104
customer benefits 4, 12, 16, 17, 31, 57, 68, 89, 92, 94, 103

departmental letters 74, 75
departmental cards 74, 75
direct mail 63, 64, 65, 66, 67, 57, 58, 59, 60, 61, 62, 63, 64, 65, 66, 67
drama 18, 19, 63, 112

emergencies 35, 36
exaggeration 15, 73

facts 7, 8, 9, 10, 11, 12, 34, 65, 66, 67, 78, 79, 89, 92, 103
focal point 19, 25, 105
formats 20, 35

generalities 9, 64, 65, 82, 83, 94, 104
gimmicks 28, 75, 76, 105

122

ABOUT THE AUTHORS:

Judy Young Ocko is probably the only retail advertising pro with a Ph.D. in Archaeology. Her first job was as copy cub under Bernice Fitzgibbon at Gimbels New York. From there she went to Bamberger's, then to an ad agency. This was followed by Divisional Ad Manager at Macy's, then Copy Chief for Gimbels. Since that time she has been a free-lance writer and advertising consultant. Mrs. Ocko's clients run from specialty stores to a symphony orchestra, from a meat packer to TV producers. She also teaches, runs copy clinics, and lectures extensively. In 1974, she was elected to the Retail Advertising Hall of Fame.

Morris L. Rosenblum, known wherever retail ads are created as "Rosy", is a graduate of Pratt Institute who made him its Alumnus of the Year in 1969. From Art Director of Abraham & Straus, he became Art and Display Director of Bamberger's. Then after 3 years as president of an advertising agency, he joined Macy's New York, becoming Vice President and Creative Director in 1965. He added Emeritus to this title in 1973. He is now consultant to large and small stores across the country. His many awards include the NRMA silver medal for his contributions to the retail industry and election to the Retail Hall of Fame. In 1972 he was Chairman of the Sales Promotion Division of NRMA.

BOOKS ON ADVERTISING

Ocko, J.Y. "Retail Advertising Copy: The How, the What, the Why'.

Rosenblum, M. L. "How to Design Effective Store Advertising".

Ocko & Rosenblum: "The Specialty Store and its Advertising. How to Plan it/How to Create it/How to Improve it".

Ocko & Rosenblum: "How to be a Retail Advertising Pro".

Ocko & Rosenblum: "Your Sale Advertising Can Be Better"